Frontier Follies

ALSO BY REE DRUMMOND

The Pioneer Woman Cooks:
The New Frontier

The Pioneer Woman Cooks:
Come and Get It!

The Pioneer Woman Cooks:
Dinnertime

The Pioneer Woman Cooks:
A Year of Holidays

The Pioneer Woman Cooks:
Food from My Frontier

The Pioneer Woman Cooks:
Recipes from an Accidental Country Girl

✱

The Pioneer Woman:
Black Heels to Tractor Wheels

Charlie the Ranch Dog series

Little Ree series

Frontier Follies

Adventures in Marriage & Motherhood in the Middle of Nowhere

Ree Drummond

HARPER LARGE PRINT

An Imprint of HarperCollinsPublishers

Hand-lettering and illustrations by Joel Holland

HarperCollins books may be purchased for educational, business, or sales promotional use. For information, please e-mail the Special Markets Department at SPsales@harpercollins.com.

FIRST HARPER LARGE PRINT EDITION

ISBN: 978-0-06-297880-6

Library of Congress Cataloging-in-Publication Data is available upon request.

20 21 22 23 24   LSC   10 9 8 7 6 5 4 3 2 1

To my funny family:
Thank you for making me laugh, smile,
roll my eyes, jump for joy, cry, rejoice,
pull my hair out, and crack up.
I love you all so much.

♡ MAMA

Contents

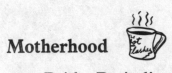

Motherhood

Introduction

I love stories of everyday life. It's why I mailed my grandma letters during my childhood when she lived only twenty minutes from my house, wrote cards to my high school friends when we all went to separate colleges, and sent my mom wordy weekly emails when my kids were still babies, once the electronic medium became a thing. Ga-Ga and my mom saved all their notes and messages and shared a pile of them with me a few years ago. I had to laugh at the kinds of things I used to scribble to them about. They were most often short anecdotes about something weird the family cat had done, funny exchanges with my brother, or quirky things I'd observed about a friend or one of the kids. It was always news, but it was simple, local news—from me, the reporter in the field.

This same penchant for sharing the everyday is exactly what drew me to blogging back in the old days, when Alex, my oldest, was just seven. (She's twenty-three now!) Daily life on our family's ranch was positively peppered with these funny stand-alone happenings, and I simply couldn't keep them in my head any longer. Thank goodness blogging came along when it did; my mom wouldn't have had room on her computer for that many emails. My grandma would have had to build a storage shed to hold all the letters.

Frontier Follies is a silly celebration of the everyday moments of my life in rural America, and every single story you'll read is true. From marital disagreements with my hunky husband (and what I do when they're going on) to out-there conversations with my mother-in-law, from disturbing incidents involving skunks and shotguns to my best friend praying the Rosary over my belly to keep me from having an epidural, I've spent the past year tapping my memory for these tales that are sure to make you chuckle (or even just feel a little better about your own wacky family).

This book is not a sustained narrative, except in the sense that love is woven throughout. Real life is woven through, too, and I share some real reflections about marriage and parenting that I hope you'll be able to relate to (particularly if you've ever had teenagers in your house . . . for an extended period of time . . . day in, day out . . . pandemic parenting, anyone?). I'm including a handful of classic stories that used to be on my blog ages ago (and added a lot more detail to them), but most of the essays in this book are new—which is what made the writing process so much fun for me. The memories and stories kept coming, and I let them pour onto the page.

To keep things up to the minute, in addition to stories from the old days of our family, I also take this opportunity to share some new, unexpected developments in the Drummond house . . . as well as things that are in the works. The timeline of this book spans almost twenty-five years, so I cover a lot of ground!

What I hope you gain from this collection of tales is a renewed sense of enjoyment over the everyday moments and laughter of life. I hope it helps you dig up some of those quirky old stories from your own family, and I sure hope it makes you smile.

Love,
Ree ♡

Marriage

LADD

Our Worst First Year

~

L add and I have the unenviable advantage of having had a really awful first year of marriage, which has made most marital years since seem like a walk in the park! Now today, at the ripe old age of I'm-not-telling (okay, fifty-one), I can put most of these newlywed struggles into perspective and say that "awful" is an exceedingly relative term. We didn't experience terrible tragedy or loss, and our basic human needs were met. But still . . . it's an interesting phenomenon to look back on one's first year of marriage with one's husband and be able to agree that it absolutely excelled at being lousy.

We had a beautiful wedding. That was the easy part. But during our honeymoon in Australia, I developed an inner ear condition (a result of the fourteen-hour flight from Los Angeles) that made me constantly dizzy and also prevented me from being able to walk in a straight line. This was slightly inconvenient for a young bride who wanted to be vivacious and glowing, but my equilibrium was kaput and I couldn't do anything about it. In addition, Ladd couldn't find anything in Australia that he (with his palate of a nine-year-old) could bear to eat, so he was baseline hangry the entire trip. We rented a car that made Clark Griswold's Family Truckster look like a Mercedes—an absolute nightmare for Ladd, who would rather not be the center of attention on any highway, especially an international one. To top it off, Ladd experienced huge losses in the commodity market over the course of two September days, which caused a sizable decrease in equity. This didn't concern me too much since I didn't really understand it, but from his perspective, it might have pulled the rug out from under his plans for starting out life on the ranch with his vivacious and glowing (not) new wife. We went home from Australia a week early.

When we got back to the ranch after our honeymoon, I found myself disoriented as a new resident of the countryside, and I had no idea where and how to get my bearings. I loved Ladd and wanted to be with him and his Wranglers more than anything, but I struggled to acclimate to my new rural reality. Horses stared at me through our bedroom window at night; I thought they were serial killers. Bobcats ransacked our trash; I'd never known this to happen during my upbringing on the golf course. A family of skunks moved in under our house; I smelled them every time they rubbed their stinky backs against the rough parts of the foundation, like a scratch-and-sniff book in hell. And the mice in the walls—they chewed and crunched on things in the night just to try to make me lose my mind. It worked.

When we were engaged, Ladd and I had talked about "letting nature take its course" once we were married, and five weeks after the big day, I found out I was pregnant. I guess Ladd and I both had missed the day in health class when these points were driven home, but somehow we both thought it would take a little longer? But it didn't, and I found myself both with child and without trash service at the exact same time in my life—a really unfortunate combination. The food aversions started before the six-week mark, then the morning sickness (which was actually all-day sickness) hit just about the time my mom called to tell me that she and my dad were getting divorced.

From there, I balanced vomiting and sobbing with driving to my hometown several times a week to check on my dad, all while my husband was working double time on the ranch to hold everything together. My poor cowboy was stressed, preoccupied, and depleted. When

I was home, I could hardly stand to cook because everything I previously loved to eat made me want to curl up in a ball and suck my thumb. Except sucking my thumb made me nauseated, so I had nowhere to go. I felt guilty for not being present for Ladd. I had serial killer horses stalking me at night. I had a flat tire every three days. The smell of laundry detergent rendered me incapable of doing laundry. There was basically no escape from queasiness, concern, and confusion over how utterly bizarre a turn my life had taken in just a few short months. Life on the ranch ticked along . . . and the mice in the walls, they kept on a-chewing.

On a very superficial note, and I'm not lumping this into the list of reasons that our first year of marriage was the worst (though it certainly didn't help my daily outlook), I wound up not being an attractive pregnant person. If Instagram had existed back then, which it blessedly did not, I would not have been one of the pregnant women who posted beautiful, hazy maternity photos with my hands making the shape of a heart over my rounded, taut belly. If I posted a maternity photo back then, it would be of me bouncing along on the John Deere riding lawn mower Ladd had given me for a wedding gift months earlier, hair in a neon pink scrunchie on top of my head, twenty pounds heavier than on my wedding day, neck sunburned, wearing a maternity T-shirt with the sleeves cut off because I was always hot. Yes, that was the sex goddess I had morphed into by May 1997, less than a year after we were married. And while Ladd was sweet about telling me all the right things, I couldn't help but wonder if he wanted a refund.

Long story short and fast-forward: Our baby Alex was born, Ladd didn't lose the ranch, my dad pulled out of the fog of the divorce and eventually remarried, and I never wore my pre-pregnancy jeans again. I don't even know what happened to them; maybe the tornado I forgot to tell you about—it also happened that first year of our marriage—blew them to another state. I hope they found a good home. We went on to have three more children, the ranch settled into a more healthy place, I started an unexpected career, and Ladd and I have always reflected (and laughed) about how far we've come from that shaky first year of matrimony, when the tears, vomit, and breast milk flowed abundantly.

You know what else is funny about our worst first year of marriage? And again, this is highly superficial: I'd absolutely kill to weigh what I weighed back then, when I was bouncing along pregnant on that John Deere riding lawnmower.

Life is interesting!

Love in the Time of Rubber Snakes

L add and I scare each other with rubber snakes. We've done this since very early in our marriage, and I don't recall exactly when or how it started. I also don't remember *who* started it. And honestly, it doesn't matter at this point; this madness has gone on for years. It's one of our primary love languages, it's how we get our kicks, and one of us is going to cause the other to have a heart attack as a result of it—which will be very hard to explain to our loved ones, but we'll cross that bridge when we come to it. Scaring each other with rubber snakes is the funniest non-funny thing in the world. Also, it's escalating.

I remember in our earlier, sweeter years, the fake snakes were made of bright, unnaturally colored rubber that smelled like swimming pool floaties, which made them seem not scary at all. One might find this kind of fake snake at dollar stores or in McDonald's Happy Meals, and they weighed about the same as a rubber band. We had so much innocent fun. I'd slip, say, a thin neon orange snake under Ladd's remote control when he wasn't looking. He'd do a double take, jerk a little, and chuckle. He'd leave a flimsy purple snake in my bathroom sink. I'd let out a cute little shriek and giggle. We'd give each other fake little arm punches, say something like "You silly goose!" or "You kidder!" and wind up in a playful hug. We were so young, so predictable, so naïve, so thin. And we were just getting warmed up.

Seasons passed, our children grew, and the snakes got larger. Bright colors were replaced with deeper, more realistic tones of ebony and moss, and we got a little craftier about our hiding places. We planted them on the shower floor so that when the unsuspecting spouse, usually naked and vulnerable, reached in to turn on the water, they'd encounter the slithering (not really, but the imagination is a powerful thing) serpent. We nestled them just under each other's pillows, so that when the other rearranged or reached underneath, they'd feel the snake and jump backward in fear and panic. I even stuck one in the freezer while filming an episode of my cooking show with Ladd, then asked him (in my best June Cleaver voice) to "grab the ice cream, please, honey?" His reaction—a very subtle, startled jump—was wonderfully juicy. That it happened to be caught on camera and recorded for posterity sustained me for months. Also, he denies that he reacted at all, which makes the memory even more fantastic for me. When he starts denying that the snake pranks affect him at all, that's when I know I'm getting under his skin.

As we veered into our forties, we started playing for keeps, and the realistic nature of our snakes skyrocketed. I started buying them from museum catalogs and educational supply stores, where anatomical accuracy in reptilian figurines is valued. They were so incredibly spot-on that it was impossible to tell they weren't real unless you picked one up, which you'd never do because you'd be too busy running out the door in fear. Our cute little "silly goose" name-calling became much more pointed. It wasn't unusual for me, at the height of a fearful snake prank reaction, to accidentally cuss or call Ladd something more hurtful. I won't go into detail, but it began with one or more of the following: M, F, A, D, P, and S.

It's important to note that Ladd and I, by virtue of our rural geography, have absolutely zero business joking around about snakes. Living in the country, snakes—from venomous water moccasins and rattle-snakes to harmless garter and king snakes—are a part of everyday life on the ranch. Ladd and I would no more walk barefoot across our yard at night than we would wade in the creek at any time of day—it's a surefire way to step on either a snake . . . or a nest of them. We see snakes sidewinding across our road, I've encountered a good five or six inside our house through the years, and I can never forget the times a rattler has had the audacity to coil up on our porch, ready to spar with our sweet striped cat. (I guess they're both competing for the same mice, so there's built-in tension?)

Anyway, what I'm saying is that if it's very unfunny to tease your partner with rubber snakes in a normal suburban setting, it is one thousand times more un-funny if you and your partner live in the country. Early on, when my mother-in-law, Nan, discovered the dys-functional snake thing Ladd and I had going on, she begged us to stop. "You're going to desensitize each other to snakes!" she'd insist. "And then when you see a real snake, you won't think it's real and you'll get bit and lose a toe! Or your whole leg!" She would often cite a corresponding example of someone losing a toe or leg that always seemed to have happened in the next county over. For the life of me, I never met any of these people. But I did stop and consider what she was saying. She had a point there.

But it hasn't played out the way she predicted at all. Instead of numbing me to the horrors and dangers of snakes, our marital shenanigans have only served to heighten my fear of them over time, and today I'm jumpier than ever. Ladd, on the other hand, seems to have plateaued in the intensity of his startled responses . . . but not, unfortunately, in the severity or cleverness of his pranks. He has progressed to borrowing stuffed rattlesnakes from his former high school football coach, who happens to own a taxidermy shop in town. And he now places them in unforgivably believable spots: in tall grass near a fence post before my evening walks, on our porch under the garden hose, in our pantry behind the flour canister. More than ever, I scream, convulse, jump, and sometimes crumble onto the ground in terror. One time I was so startled that I kicked the taxidermy rattlesnake across the room—a curious reaction, considering I don't think I'd ever kick an actual rattlesnake—which caused its scales to break off in sheets. I am still avoiding calling Coach DeMoss to apologize, tell him what happened, and pay for the ruined snake, although I really feel that legally, Ladd should be the one to pay. I think my case is strong here.

Another strange offshoot of this madness is that I am now regularly, inadvertently scaring *myself* with rubber snakes; I don't even seem to need Ladd anymore. Sometimes I plant one for him to find, then stumble upon it myself before he has a chance to. Or I stick a snake in a drawer for safekeeping, then open the drawer five minutes later, forgetting I've put it there. At this point, I'll jump and scream if I see a belt on a hanger. I startle and shriek at twigs in the yard. Before too long, I'll probably be terrified of dental floss. What will become of my gum health?

There's one thing, however, that still happens no matter what, when, where, or how the snake prank occurs. Ladd and I somehow always wind up in a hug— even if the hug was preceded by my punching him (and not a fake little punch anymore) in the arm. We're still raising our kids, we're swamped with ranching, work, and sports, and our to-do lists are unrelenting. But the weird snake thing has always been a touchstone for us—a way for us to connect and remind each other that while we're getting a little long in the tooth, the monkey business of our younger marriage is still very much alive.

I can't wait for the next stage of our snake dysfunction. Anyone have a rubber anaconda I can borrow?

Places to Hide Rubber Snakes (for Your Favorite Sweetheart to Find)

A simple way to add a little spark to your marriage!

* Freezer
* Produce drawer
* Mailbox
* Behind the cereal
* Sock drawer
* Top rack of the dishwasher
* Purse
* Briefcase
* Washing machine
* Inside a pot (with the lid on!)
* Under the garden hose
* In a flowerpot
* Hanging from a doorknob
* Inside a packed suitcase
* Under a pillow
* In the shower
* Inside a boot
* Under the covers near the end of the bed (feet!)

Have fun! ☺

I Do Dishes
When We Argue

Like most couples who've been married nearly half their lives, Ladd and I have occasional arguments. Now, I definitely wouldn't characterize us as a quarrelsome couple; I don't thrive on fighting in relationships, I don't enjoy drama, and I tend to be a peacemaker . . . most of the time. Ladd is a little more confrontational in the sense that if he feels we need to talk about something, work something out, or come to an understanding, he wants to do it right then and there, when the issue comes up and the feelings are fresh. He doesn't believe in ruminating and festering, which is really annoying considering I do. Or better yet: I would rather just ignore the conflict and let it float away into the ether and disappear. Which one of us is healthier? Never mind, don't answer that.

Early in our marriage, whenever a disagreement or argument would happen, I started noticing the most bizarre thing: I would mindlessly migrate into the kitchen and start doing dishes right in the middle of it. It didn't matter if we were in the garage—or heck, outside in a pasture—when the tiff began. Just a few terse sentences in, and I would suddenly find myself standing at the sink, suds up to my elbows, pouring every ounce of my passion into getting the last bit of grime off each dish. If I ran out of dishes before the "discussion" was over, I'd grab a clean dish and wash it again. Only when we resolved the issue or otherwise stopped the conversation did I turn off the water and declare that the dishes finally, at long last, were clean.

The thing is, I don't even like washing dishes. It isn't anything I've ever remotely enjoyed. I despise it, actually, and Ladd knows this. It's a tedious and repetitive task, I have to stand still in one spot, and my fingers get pruny. But for some reason, during those marital arguments, washing dishes very quickly becomes my favorite pastime, my most cherished hobby—my life's work, really. (It's important to note that I have two perfectly functioning automatic dishwashers.)

So here's the thing: I noticed this washing-dishes-during-arguments anomaly a good five years before

Ladd did. It was my own little secret with myself. I'd look at the rack of brilliantly clean dishes and marvel at how quickly I'd knocked them out, during just a brief dispute with my husband. It both amazed and amused me. Sometimes I'd even laugh about it, putting my hand over my mouth lest Ladd inquire about what was so funny. But then one day, out of the blue, just around the time of our seven-year itch, my husband recognized the pattern. And the reason I knew he'd figured it out is because (in true Ladd tell-it-like-it-is form) he *told* me he'd figured it out. He actually confronted me about it during a confrontation! "How come," he inquired that evening, mid-disagreement, "you *always* start doing dishes whenever we have a fight?"

I played dumb, of course. "Well, I don't really think we're fighting, are we?" (I'm so bad at playing dumb.)

"Fighting, arguing, talking, debating—whatever," he said. "You always come in here and start doing dishes."

"I do dishes every day," I began . . . but quickly gave up. "Okay, yes. You're right. I do dishes when we fight."

"I know. I just said that," my beloved responded.

"I know you just said that," I replied. "But I said I know because I already knew that I did that. Y'know?"

"Wait . . . what?" Ladd asked, confused. Arguing with me is very weird. I'm like a moving target, except I don't really move. I just kind of stand there, do dishes, and say confusing things. And by then we're so mixed up, we can't even remember what we were arguing about, so my unintentionally wicked plan usually works!

Except, of course, for the time the sink had piled up with dishes beyond what is normal or acceptable in civilized society. It had just been one of those months— I'm kidding! It had just been one of those days where I was so busy and my momentum took me in a different direction. So by 7:00 p.m., with the care of four children tugging at my energy level, I was about to turn off the kitchen light and just ignore the dishes until morning. But then Ladd, back from the barn, walked into the kitchen to get some water and glanced at the kitchen sink. Admittedly, it was an aberration. It was shocking. It was packed with dishes to the ceiling. It looked like something I'd seen on TLC shows or *Jerry Springer*. Too tired to be bothered, I was fine to leave it and go get some beauty sleep.

But Ladd saw an opportunity. He laughed and made light of it by suggesting that maybe he should pick a fight, because then the dishes would surely get done.

I divorced him on the spot. Not really, but I did murder him on the spot. Not really, but it briefly crossed my mind. Then I laughed, because . . . to tell you the truth, it was actually pretty funny. We wound up doing the dishes together that night, which was a nice little end to that marital moment. And fortunately, so far in our relationship, that's how our problems usually wind up getting resolved: with a laugh or a chuckle over the inherent humor of the situation, or just the inherent humor of life. Add in a little exhaustion and the perspective that comes with being together for twenty-five years, and we're generally too tired or chill to argue these days. Fatigue: the secret to a happy marriage!

Still, over the years I've tried to analyze this dishwashing strangeness of mine, which continues to this day whenever issues come up between my beloved and me. Why *do* I do dishes when we argue? I can't decide whether I think of the fine soapy suds as a barrier between me and the (albeit temporary) moment of marital strife, or as some kind of disinfectant that will wash away all the unpleasantness of the moment. Or do I just not like sitting down, making eye contact, and hashing things out? As much as I hate doing dishes, maybe I hate that more? Or maybe, given the fact that I hate doing dishes so much, I consider it some kind of sacrifice or penance—an offering up of myself for the greater good of my marriage?

Whatever the reason, conscious or unconscious, my dishwashing idiosyncrasy is at least a handy one to possess. If I could just short-circuit it from time to time and move our arguments to the laundry room . . .

All I Wanted Was a Doughnut

A couple of days before Christmas many years ago, Ladd and I decided to run to the big city to shop for his mom and grandma, to grab a couple of last-minute gifts for the kids, and to be alone together and have one-on-one conversations without our four precious children or our demanding cattle herd needing something from us. Or was it our four demanding children or our precious cattle herd needing something from us? The lines are blurred sometimes. And we didn't "run" to the big city, we drove, which brings me to the point of this story. Part of the conversation in Ladd's pickup on our trip to the city that day was our just-formed winter-time plan of getting me back into shape. It was to start the following morning and involved getting out of bed at 5:00 a.m. so that we could spend an hour working out together before the kids had to get up and before Ladd had to go feed cattle. This entire conversation had begun twenty minutes earlier, when I started lamenting how tight my jeans had become after a summer and fall of cooking constantly for a cookbook I was working on, filming my new cooking show, and discovering how much I loved semisoft, unripe cheese.

"I'm to the point," I whined, "that I need to either buy bigger jeans or make smarter choices about what I eat! And I need to exercise, for gosh sake." And then I really let Ladd have it: "I have back fat!" I sat back in the passenger seat, relieved to have gotten the rant out.

Ladd, calmly and without agreeing with my back fat lamentation, began to lay out his prescription for me: early morning exercise to boost my metabolism and start the day off right. To sweeten the pot, he committed to joining me in my new fitness regimen so I wouldn't have to go it alone. This was nice of him, but I could tell he didn't empathize with me at all. He is, after all, chiseled out of granite and weighs the same as he did when he was seventeen. I would be really annoyed with him if I wasn't so attracted to him.

Two-thirds of the way to the big city, I asked Ladd to pull off the highway and stop at a very busy convenience store called Quik Trip, so I could get some coffee. I was getting over a cold and had been feeling a little draggy, plus the conversation about my getting up at five to exercise for an hour had really worn me out. He pulled into the parking lot and we both went inside; Ladd headed straight to the refrigerated section to get a can of Dr Pepper while I headed to the coffee section to fill a large cup of joe for myself.

It took me a while to fill my cup, because this particular convenience store has an especially beautiful run of coffee options. You can get French roast, Colombian roast, breakfast blend, Kona blend . . . not to mention all sorts of little squirts of flavor and shots of different incarnations of creamer. I want this coffee area in my house, is what I'm saying. So anyway, I stood there and decanted, squirted, and decanted some more until I had a great big cup of luscious convenience store coffee that was likely extremely caloric, but I had only one more day before my new exercise program was to begin, so I figured I'd go out with a bang.

I headed toward the register. I could see Ladd standing there waiting for me so he could pay for his pop and my coffee together, because he's chivalrous like that, and also because he has never known me to have a single dollar of cash on my person. The store was packed with other patrons, and along my journey to the front, I passed Quik Trip's very large, very impressive, very alluring glass doughnut case and made the mistake of glancing in its direction. I immediately locked eyes with an apple fritter on the top shelf. It hypnotized me instantly, then reached out its long, evil fingers and said, "Come . . . come to me." Quik Trip's apple fritters are so freaking good. I'm powerless in their presence. Those crisp, craggy edges . . . oh my!

Without thinking, I removed an individual square of paper from the dispenser on the service shelf below, then reached for the knob of the glass door that was separating me from my apple fritter boyfriend. I say "without thinking" because I somehow had completely pushed out of my consciousness the entire back fat conversation I'd just had with Ladd minutes earlier. Or maybe I just rationalized it by reminding myself that I only had the rest of the day to party before my 5:00 a.m. boot camp began . . . or maybe I temporarily convinced myself that apple fritters are actually a healthy doughnut option? They have fruit in them, after all.

For whatever reason, I pulled the knob to the right, thinking the door would slide to open, but instead it met with resistance. I had Christmas shopping on my mind—what size top I should get Ladd's grandma, Edna Mae, and how I couldn't wait to sniff all the men's cologne at the perfume counter—and I inexplicably pulled backward on the knob, possibly thinking that the door opened by flipping up rather than sliding to the side. Then, with zero warning, a terrifying sound crashed through the heavily trafficked convenience store and I realized that the entire tempered glass façade of the big, impressive doughnut case had shattered into four hundred million tiny, sparkly pieces. The sound was deafening and seemed to happen in slow motion, as if a house of glass sitting on a frozen lake had fallen down wall by wall. I stood there in shock, not knowing what to do. Glass was everywhere: all over the doughnuts, littering the floor, in the adjacent sandwich case, and in my boots, into which I'd tucked my pant legs that morning. The small stainless steel knob was still in my hand. I stood there, completely stunned.

Customers ran over to see what had happened, my husband among them. And when Ladd saw me standing there in the middle of a sea of tempered glass, a small knob in my hand, the now-unprotected array of doughnuts right in front of me, not to mention the look of horror and confusion on my face, he had but two questions:

"Are you okay?

"Yes."

"What happened?"

"I wanted a doughnut."

By now the manager, assistant manager, cashier, assistant cashier, and probably all their friends and relatives had rushed to the scene. The manager wanted first to make sure I was okay.

"Ma'am, are you all right?" the nice gentleman said. "You're not hurt, are you?"

Still holding the knob, I answered, "Yes. My pride is hurt. It is badly, badly injured."

But other than that, I told him, I was totally fine, and might I please borrow a broom and shop vac so I could whisk all this away and pretend it never happened? I noticed another female customer out of the corner of my eye. She had her hand over her mouth.

"Oh, we'll take care of it," the manager said. "I just wanted to make sure you're okay."

"I'm absolutely fine," I insisted. "I am so, so sorry. I don't know what happened. One minute I was reaching for an apple fritter . . . the next minute . . ." I shook my head in disbelief.

"It's perfectly okay, ma'am," he reassured me. "This has actually happened once before."

I immediately felt better. I wasn't the only person who'd shattered the doughnut case at this convenience store. What a relief! All was suddenly better now.

But then I did something I can't explain. I instinctively began reaching for the apple fritter, still in the shattered case. I don't think I actually had any control over this action. I didn't logically believe I should get the apple fritter; I think it was a desperate attempt just to carry on and pretend the whole thing hadn't happened. Well, and I guess I really just wanted a doughnut.

That's when the assistant manager stepped in. "Oh, ma'am . . . ," she said, "you can't have a doughnut now."

I know she was just trying to protect my gastrointestinal tract from glass shards, but at the time she said it I felt like a little girl who had just been grounded from eating doughnuts. My face felt hot.

After several minutes of offering to help clean up and insisting on paying for the broken glass and trying to figure out what country I was going to move to once I left the store, I made my way to the front counter so that Ladd could finally pay for my coffee. But when we got there, the cashier held up his hand and said, "Don't worry about it—no charge." I think he wanted me to leave the store as soon as humanly possible.

When we got into Ladd's pickup and continued on our trip to the big city, I glanced over at him. He had a look on his face that I'll never be able to describe. It was the look of a husband who is married to a complete klutz who complains about her tight jeans then stops at a convenience store to buy sugary coffee and shatters a doughnut case while trying to retrieve an eight-hundred-calorie apple fritter. It was the look of a husband who has seen his wife fall down, run into doors, use the wrong remote control to change channels on the TV, and wear her black leggings inside out for an entire day without knowing. It was the look of a husband who had just filed another incident into his vault of similar moments . . . and who couldn't wait to remind me of it the next time we're driving together and I say I want to pull over and get coffee.

"You're . . . funny," he said, reaching over and squeezing my knee.

Poor guy can't take me anywhere.

My Top Five Favorite Forms of Exercise

1. *Pilates.* It relaxes me and makes me feel strong. (When I do it.)

2. *Rowing machine.* I love sitting down when I exercise! I pretend I'm in Rob Lowe's boat in *Oxford Blues.*

3. *Walking with the dogs.* I listen to murder podcasts and scare myself, then have to call Ladd to come down the road and pick me up.

4. *Jane Fonda's Workout.* The 1982 original. I'd kill for that pink-and-purple striped leotard.

5. *Ballet.* My first fitness love. I pretend I'm onstage in *The Nutcracker* and all my ex-boyfriends are in the audience!

My Top Five Favorite Kinds of Doughnuts

1. *Apple Fritter.* But only from Quik Trip. Preferably with no glass shards.

2. *Old-Fashioned.* I break off the four sides and eat them one by one.

3. *Maple Long John.* Preferably with really thick maple icing that gets all over my fingers.

4. *Chocolate-Glazed Old-Fashioned.* With rainbow sprinkles, please.

5. *Apple Fritter.* They deserve a second mention!

Ladd and the Gala

few things about Ladd and food:

1. He likes beef.

2. He likes potatoes.

3. He likes to eat, not dine. Prolonged multicourse meal experiences are his worst nightmare.

Another thing about Ladd: He suffers from a troubling (for me) condition called Low Blood Sugar Cranky Butt Disorder, or LBSCBD for short. I identified this affliction early in our marriage, and I believe it is a very real condition that should be named in the *New England Journal of Medicine* so that a cure can soon be found. If Ladd does not eat when he (or any human) typically should eat, his mood plummets and he becomes a shorter, terser, more temperamental version of his cute, charming, Wrangler-wearing self.

I should also point out that if Ladd and I ever have the chance to go out to a restaurant for a nice meal, which is approximately once every forty-seven years, he makes it a practice to completely abstain from food for the entire day leading up to the meal. I can't imagine going three hours without eating, so the concept is foreign to me, but his thinking is that by doing this, (a) he'll have a much more guilt-free eating experience because he hasn't consumed any other calories that day, and (b) he'll be so hungry by the time he eats his meal, it will taste that much more delicious. Again, we hardly ever go out to eat. Ladd wants every moment of it to count.

Problems in the world (and in our marriage) arise when you add Ladd's pre-dinner-date abstinence and his LBSCBD together. By the time we are finally on our way to the eating establishment (usually at least an hour away from the ranch), Ladd hasn't eaten and is veering very quickly toward crankdom. Usually the hope of the coming meal buoys his mood enough to sustain him until the bread basket gets set on the table, so while I wouldn't describe our pre-date car conversation as energetic or chatty, I appreciate that he is able to grin and bear it and not come completely unraveled. Again, I never deny myself food, so I can't relate to this bizarre practice at all. If my stomach so much as growls on the way to a dinner date, I'll pull over to a McDonald's and order some fries.

With all of the above in mind, Ladd and I were invited to a charity gala many years ago. We aren't gala types—in fact, this would be the first gala my husband had ever attended in his life—but my sweet stepmother Patsy happened to be the director of the performing arts center where the gala was taking place, and she and my dad invited us to join them at their table. So one Saturday night, following a morning and afternoon of Ladd denying himself all food because of the promise of a big dinner, we got dressed up in black and headed toward Gala Land. Ladd was strangely excited! He never loved dressing in a suit, but because of our middle-of-America geography, he predicted that either prime rib or beef tenderloin lay ahead—an educated guess given that beef usually has a significant presence at weddings and other catered events in our region of the country. After the long drive from the ranch and an hour-long cocktail reception (with tiny, frilly canapés he politely passed on), he was more than ready for a big, hearty supper.

When we finally sat down to our table, I knew things

might be headed south. Our first course, the appetizer, had already been placed on the table. Imagine if you will a cowboy who thinks the sun rises and sets on a steak and a baked potato, and imagine he's so hungry that he can no longer concentrate on what's going on in the room around him. Then imagine that he sits down to eat and sees in front of him a shiny white plate with two silver-dollar-sized crostini—one spread with an artichoke puree and one spread with tomato compote. While such food delights and excites me, it is nothing that Ladd would ever in a million years place inside his mouth. First, it's too small. Second, it's topped with mushy substances that are unrecognizable. Third . . . no. He didn't want to appear rude, however, so he waited until I ate both of mine, then stealthily slipped his crostini onto my plate. (Ever the dutiful wife, I went ahead and ate them. I didn't want to appear rude, either.)

The second course arrived: roasted squash gazpacho with an anchovy fillet. Heaven for me, hell for Ladd, and again, I quickly slurped down his helping. His normally soft blue eyes turned ice cold. He loosened his tie as he exhaled. Third course: watercress salad consisting of five leaves. Ladd normally likes salad—but there wasn't any ranch dressing on it, and they forgot the iceberg lettuce. This was some kind of Greek tragedy!

I could hear his stomach rumbling. It sounded like the *T. rex* in *Jurassic Park*. My man wanted to be fed. Any attempt to put on a happy face was now gone with the previous course's dishes. I gave him a compassionate glance as I gobbled down his watercress.

The fourth course was the last straw: it was lacquered salmon, and Ladd eats neither lacquer nor salmon. That was it. He couldn't take it anymore. "They're actually trying to kill me, aren't they?" he whispered in my ear. He wasn't joking. His hunger level had stripped him of all clear thinking and paranoia was officially setting in. This whole thing—this "gala"—was all a conspiracy now, an evil plan hatched by my dad's darling wife and her evil board of directors. They knew Ladd, the cattle rancher, would be coming to the dinner. And they put crostini and shiny fish on the menu just to watch him in agony. It was all finally becoming clear to him. How could people be so cruel?

Giving the whole "good sport" thing one final try, Ladd took a small, half-hearted bite of his salmon at the same time I took a large, wholehearted bite of mine. I found it delicious, though decidedly fishy. The glaze was an explosion of flavors and very spicy—a recipe for disaster for my husband's steak-and-potato palate. He leaned in again, resting his hand on my shoulder: "I'll be right back," his sexy voice whispered in my ear. He got a little glaze on my earlobe, but I decided not to dwell on it.

"Where are you going?" I asked.

"McDonald's," he answered.

Honestly, I wasn't shocked at all. Relieved was more like it. That man had to eat, and he wasn't going to be able to eat as long as he stayed at the gala. I seriously couldn't bear the torture of watching him navigate this meal any longer.

"Oh my gosh, go," I whispered, reassuring him. "I'll cover for you." My dad and Patsy were making the rounds, only returning to our table for moments here and there. They would never know he had left, and he'd probably be back from McDonald's within twenty minutes if he didn't get stopped for speeding.

I had something else to tell him before he left. "And don't worry, honey," I whispered. "I'll finish the rest of your food to make sure no one suspects a thing." He didn't hear that last part because he was already peeling out of the parking lot, probably laying some serious scratch on the pavement. Ladd left just in time to miss almond-encrusted pork tenderloin with an herbed grit cake, which I thoroughly enjoyed. Soon he would be sinking his teeth into a quarter pounder with cheese and driving back my way. All was working out as it should.

Just then my dad came over to the table with a very important-looking gentlemen who happened to be wearing a cowboy hat. He was a benefactor of the performing arts center, and he wanted to meet Ladd, whom he'd pegged as a fellow cowboy earlier in the evening. My dad looked around the table, and then around the room. "Where's Ladd?" he asked quizzically. "Bathroom," I said. My dad was satisfied with this explanation, and he and Benny Factor said they'd be back by in a bit. I was actually enjoying scarfing down double portions of the gala dinner. At what point in my life would I ever again have this opportunity and be able to call it a marital service?

Long story short, Ladd returned to the gala no less than forty-three minutes after he'd departed for the Golden Arches. When I saw him enter the room, he had a glowing light of joy all about him, a look of culinary contentment on his face. He slipped into his seat as if he'd been gone only a few moments and casually joined the various circles of table conversation that were already taking place. Unfortunately, I was just finishing my own slice of Chantilly cake and hadn't had a chance to wolf down Ladd's . . . so he went ahead and dove into his piece. Finally, something at the gala that he could eat! If only they'd served the cake as the starter course.

I studied my husband for a second and immediately knew something was up, because (a) he had been gone for almost forty-five minutes, and (b) he looked almost drunk with happiness. "How was McDonald's?" I whispered, leaning close to his chiseled shoulder. "And what's her name?!?" I didn't really say that last part, but the point is—he was acting suspicious. That's when my beloved laid it on me that in the span of time he'd been absent, he'd managed to find a nice steak house, sit down, order and polish off a medium-rare rib eye and baked potato, pay his tab and a 25 percent tip, and arrive back at the gala just in time for dessert. He was almost manic as he quietly relayed his coup to me— probably the result of both having filled his stomach with satisfying food after a long famine *and* having pulled off the perfect crime.

As for me, I had a great evening. I was able to get out with my husband, wear a black dress, have adult conversation, and eat what was, in my opinion, really delicious food.

(I even got two of each helping!)

Cheatin' Movies

L add and I love movies. This (among other things) attracted us to each other while we were dating, and watching some kind of movie together is still our favorite way to spend a Saturday night. (Or any night!) And while my fella and I are aligned on most cinematic genres (except action; I don't think they make 'em like they used to), Ladd regularly points out something he has noticed about me, his wife: I have a penchant for watching "cheatin' movies." Without admitting guilt, I will first define the terms.

Cheatin': *marital infidelity.*
Movie: *a cinematic motion picture.*
Cheatin' movie: *a cinematic motion picture in which marital infidelity is often glorified or celebrated.*

Let me defend myself: I do not in any way, shape, or form set out to find cheatin' movies to watch. I do not endorse cheatin' as a healthy practice, either. It's just that I love a lot of movies, and some of them—by no fault of my own—just happen to have a storyline involving cheatin'. Can I help it if Hollywood occasionally romanticizes infidelity—or that I actually fall for it? It's not my fault.

Let me defend myself again: I have never cheated on Ladd—not when we dated, not while married. I can say with confidence that I will never cheat on Ladd. And not that physical attractiveness in any way insulates a person from being cheated on . . . but please look at the Wrangler-wearing ridiculous deliciousness that is my husband. To quote the beautiful, incomparable Whitney Houston, Ladd is all the man that I need. And also, I'm tired. Where would I find the energy?

No—cheatin' movies, for me, are all about the acting! And the writing. And the cinematography, of course. I can't help it if the movie industry doesn't honor the sacrament of marriage, and I'm not willing to boycott an otherwise lovely, entertaining movie just because one of the characters happens to stray. If Ladd continues to give me trouble about this, I will be forced to start giving him trouble about all the movies he watches that involve car theft. I'll just start calling them stealin' movies! He doesn't want to go toe to toe with me on that.

Back to cheatin' movies, though: Here are some examples. I love them; Ladd hates them. And we both lived happily ever after.

The Age of Innocence is high on my list of the greatest cheatin' movies of all time. Based on the 1920 Edith Wharton novel, this Scorsese-directed masterpiece chronicles a character named Newland Archer (played by the highly dishy and intense Daniel Day-Lewis) who is engaged to sweet, pure May (Winona Ryder) but obsessed with Countess Olenska (Michelle Pfeiffer). The whole angsty tale is just painful and luscious to watch—Newland loves May and knows in his head she is the right choice for him, but the scandal-ridden countess is just too alluring for him to resist, and they ultimately share an all-body, groan-ridden, slightly cringy kiss before the countess calls things off for fear of hurting sweet, pure May, *her beloved first cousin*! Newland does wind up marrying May but continues to obsess over the countess, and a couple of years into marriage, he finally works up the courage to leave May . . . but not before she tells him she's pregnant. *The Age of Innocence* is so great for kindergartners! Just kidding. I can't pass up the opportunity to watch it, and Ladd can't bear to watch five minutes of it. Newland needs to be a man, my husband huffs, and stop trying to straddle two worlds! (Ladd is such a buzzkill.)

Violets Are Blue is another one: It's a little-known 1986 movie that stars Sissy Spacek and oh-so-dreamy Kevin Kline, and it is absolutely awful . . . and so romantic! Sissy and Kevin are high school sweethearts whose plans for the future are interrupted both by her ambition to travel the world as a photojournalist and by the fact that he "accidentally" fathered the child of another woman—the nice girl next door, played by Bonnie Bedelia.

So here's where the cheatin' comes in, and it is egregious: Thirteen years after high school, Sissy returns to her small, coastal hometown to visit her parents for the first time since she left. And of course, she bumps into Kevin, who is now happily married to Bonnie (with whom he shares a now-teenage boy) and running his father's newspaper. In a nutshell, Kevin invites Sissy over to his family's home for dinner, Bonnie makes them all gazpacho, then Sissy says good night and starts to walk home. It's about to rain, so good-hearted Bonnie tells her nice, trustworthy husband to walk Sissy home. It's the right thing to do, after all.

So on the walk home, Sissy has a meltdown and starts crying because Kevin has a home and a family that he obviously loves, and Sissy doesn't even have a cat. Then they start arguing. Then they start yelling. Then they start kissing. Ultimately they wind up "re-uniting" under the pier just a few paces away from her destination.

Kevin! Why???

The pier incident begins a plunge-back-into-the-past affair that culminates in Kevin facing the choice of whether to abandon his family and go travel the world as Sissy's journalistic sidekick . . . or to remain in the honorable—but somewhat mundane—life he's chosen. You'll have to watch the movie to see which life he winds up choosing, but my favorite line of the movie is when Bonnie finds out that Kevin's been unfaithful and is considering leaving his small town for a more exciting life with his old flame: "If you want to go, go. I can't compete with her. But I'm not going to apologize for liking it here!" You tell him, Bonnie!

(See, Ladd? I root for the wronged spouse some-times, too. Also, Sissy Spacek has never looked more beautiful.) Ladd absolutely loathes *Violets Are Blue.*

Cousins is another absolutely blatant cheatin' movie. It's about a woman, played by Isabella Rossellini, who is more radiant than I ever thought possible, and who's in an unhappy marriage with a philandering husband. It's also about a man, Ted Danson, who's in an un-happy marriage as well with a vivacious (and, it turns out, philandering) woman. True to form, Isabella's husband and Ted's wife hook up behind the bushes at an extended family wedding after having just met, which leaves Isabella and Ted searching in vain for their respective rides home. They strike up a friendship, both quietly aware of their spouses' dalliance, and wind up spending a beautiful weekend together in a lakeside cabin doing nothing but lamenting their spouses' cheatin' . . . while also cheatin' (together) on their spouses. It's such a heartwarming movie, and Ladd still hasn't forgiven me for making him watch it.

However, the Big Kahuna of all cheatin' movies—absolutely the most unapologetic, flagrant example—is *Same Time, Next Year.* In this particular flick, Alan Alda and Ellen Burstyn play characters who are married to other people but who have an "accidental" (oops!) affair at a cliffside hotel when they're both traveling away from home one weekend. They love their spouses (obviously!) but feel such a connection with each other that they agree to meet at the same hotel at the (wait for it) *same time next year*!

Naturally, the affair continues through the decades, and the movie does do a beautiful job of portraying the passage of time from the 1950s to the 1970s in America, and all the changes both of their families go through during that time. And while it's a total burr in the saddle of anyone who values fidelity in a relationship, it does us all the favor of at least acknowledging through the course of the movie that Alan's and Ellen's spouses are real human beings who have done nothing to warrant having their husband and wife cheat on them once a year.

Unfortunately, Alda and Burstyn are so incredibly charming in *Same Time, Next Year* and have such a burning—yet still innocent and likable—chemistry that it's impossible not to come away from the movie cheering for them. But you still cheer for their spouses, too! That is the brilliance of this whole sordid film, and Ladd almost insisted that I go to marriage counseling after I asked him to watch it with me once, because I told him that "it really is such a smart, sweet movie." He completely sided with Alan's and Ellen's betrayed spouses and asked me to articulate what on God's green earth was smart and sweet about two married people perpetuating a decades-long lie. I didn't really have a good answer, but I'm still working on it.

And that's when I decided to keep my cheatin' movies to myself and watch them alone. Ladd and I share a house, four children, a ranch, and an entire life . . . but we don't have to share TVs!

The Love Robot

During the first semester of my freshman year in college, I went to a Halloween party with my roommate. She and I had lived together for a couple of months by then, and had already become good friends, so the thought of dressing up and heading out to a party to meet new people sounded like a great way to spend an evening. My roommate dressed up as Satan in a cute little red satin number; I dressed up as a cat, which consisted only of black Guess jeans (zipper ankle), a black Gap turtleneck, and whiskers drawn on my face with Estée Lauder eyeliner. My roomie and I made plans to meet up with her new love interest, Mikey, at the party, and we were so excited for the big time that lay ahead!

I wasn't at the party five minutes when I decided that rather than speak, I was just going to meow the rest of the night. It started out subtly enough: A friend I bumped into looked at me and said, "Oh! A cat! Awesome! Meow!" and walked away. I quietly answered, "Meow." She didn't hear me, of course, but that didn't matter to me. I continued to walk all over the frat house, meowing whenever someone looked in my direction. I did not utter a human word the rest of the night. If someone stopped to chat, I'd string together several meows, putting emphases on various ones so it would sound conversational. Some people laughed and moved on. Other people looked at me like I was troubled and moved on. And I didn't really care what reactions I was getting; I just knew I was fully committed to my feline character and nothing was going to cause me to quit. A cute blond frat boy bumped into me and sloshed his drink, and I hissed angrily and made a violent clawing gesture. "Jesus," he muttered as he walked away.

The pressure to break character grew as the evening went on. Mid-party, my roommate tracked me down and asked if I'd seen Mikey anywhere, as he hadn't shown up at the designated spot at the designated time. "Meow, meow," I shrugged, looking puzzled. "Meow meowmeowmeow meow-meow?" I pointed to the next room, nonverbally intimating that perhaps that's where he was. She huffed off, unamused. Sometime later she returned, still not having found Mikey, and asked me if I'd seen her car keys, because she couldn't find them and wanted to leave. "Meow," I replied, shrugging. "Meow-meow, meow meow meow-meow?" She told me she was serious and to please stop meowing, and I simply exclaimed, "Meow!" then started purring. That was the final straw for my roommate (and, now, former friend), and she got a ride home with an acquaintance. The next morning she told me unequivocally (and understandably) that my refusal to answer her questions the night before really irritated her, and she didn't want to go to any more parties with me.

All this to say that given the circumstance, I can fully commit to being completely annoying, even past the point when it affects relationships. Case in point: the Love Robot.

First, I'll back up and tell you that as my kids were growing up, I was generally a silly, wannabe comedic mom. Typically, I'd do most of my cutting up in the kitchen, since that's where I spent most of my time, laying on a thick Italian accent as I was making *meat-a-balls* (meatballs) or doing an interpretive dance to the tune of "Hotel California" as I seasoned soup. My sole motivation for being kooky was to get laughs from my kids, because they're tough nuts to crack and I figured if they laughed at me, I must be really funny. So as long as their giggling continued, my goofing off continued. It was a great way to make the years go by faster.

Over time, I started noticing that for all my dancing and impersonating, nothing caused the kids to laugh harder than the times I made Ladd the subject of my shenanigans. I started out doing the typical things: Ladd would be talking to the kids and I'd park behind him, making funny faces and mimicking his gestures, stopping instantly if he became suspicious and turned around to look. Or I'd steal his toast and hide it right after he spread the butter on, as he turned to get the strawberry preserves out of the fridge. He'd spend a few seconds looking around, completely puzzled, and the kids would laugh so hard they'd cry. Such wonderful memories at Ladd's expense!

The Love Robot showed up unexpectedly one dark and stormy night. I'd just finished cooking chili, and Ladd and the kids were filling their bowls at the stove and taking their seats at the island. Just for kicks, I suddenly shouted, "Oh my gosh! *Wait!!*" I stared at Ladd with huge eyes, my hand over my mouth, as if something dire had just happened. The kids jumped. Ladd, startled, whipped his head around and said, "What's wrong?!" He almost dropped his chili bowl.

I relaxed my face and grinned. "You forgot to give

me my hug today," I replied. The kids, realizing nothing was really the matter, roared.

Ladd shook his head and tried not to laugh, then took his bowl to his seat and sat down . . . *without giving me a hug,* mind you. This didn't initially bother me, but then I thought about it and wondered why he hadn't just played along and given me a hug. I mean, it was no big deal. But it was a big deal. But it wasn't. But it was. So almost without thinking, I stiffened my body upright, extended my arms in front of me at a ninety-degree angle with my forearms parallel to the floor, and began shuffling toward my husband just as a metal-encased robot would.

Bryce noticed my change of character right away. "What are you doing, Mama?" he asked in his cute little voice.

I chose a monotone one-note beep of a voice and held my head absolutely straight: "I am . . . the Love Robot . . . ," I replied. "I . . . must have love . . . I . . . must have . . . hug . . ." When I made it over to Ladd, I continued walking toward him until my legs hit his barstool. My feet still shuffled, as if I were a battery-operated car that got hung up in the corner of the room with the wheels still spinning. Ladd, wanting so badly to enjoy a relaxing dinner, tried to ignore me while spreading honey butter on his corn muffin, hoping to

God it would stop. Unfortunately, it only made me dig in. He was by this time completely trapped between my rigid robot arms, so I folded them inward in a repeated motion, just as a robot would give a series of stiff hugs. Ladd, still trying hard to act unfazed and eat his damn chili, was now visibly trying to restrain himself from laughing. He could not under any circumstances give the Love Robot the satisfaction. The kids, on the other hand, were howling.

"Hug me . . . ," I continued, begging in my robot voice for him to hug me back. "Love Robot . . . need love . . ." I kept my short-circuited robot hugs going until Ladd placated me with a little pat on the arm. "Okay, let's eat," he said gently . . . though I noticed his jaw muscle was clenching a little bit. I guess he'd had a hard day on the ranch and just wanted to have a simple meal with his family? So I shuffled backward, turned around 180 degrees, and shuffled over to the stove to serve myself some chili, never for a second breaking character.

The rest of dinner was awkward but fun. The kids interrogated the Love Robot about where I came from, what my mother's name was, and how long I was going to stay in the house with them. All the while, I ate chili and cornbread muffins using only up-and-down or side-to-side movements with my head and hands. Consequently, the Love Robot made quite a royal mess, which brought the kids great delight as well. (Have you ever seen a robot try to eat chili? It's hilarious!) And poor Ladd: Turns out he actually had some things he'd wanted to talk to his wife and kids about over dinner— ranching plans for the week and whatnot—but a robot had possessed his wife's body and was answering only in one-tone beeps. Oh, was I committed. It was just like the Halloween party in college. (Only with slightly larger jeans.)

As I normally would, I cleared the table, did the dishes, and wiped the countertops, all the while in full Love Robot character. Interestingly, everyone else trickled out of the kitchen one by one. Once I realized they were gone, I announced, in my own special robotic way, that I was about to run out of power and needed a hug immediately in order to keep my batteries from dying. I even turned off the kitchen lights, tilted forward forty-five degrees, and stayed there, frozen, announcing every thirty seconds or so that the Love Robot was out of power and "must . . . have hugs . . . must . . . have love . . ." in order to come back to life.

I stayed there a little too long, because I actually strained my lower back from freezing in a bent position, hoping someone would come charge my—I mean the Love Robot's—batteries by giving me a hug. By this time, though, everyone had settled in to watch TV in the living room for the evening and they sort of left me out to dry. It didn't really hurt my feelings, since I had started the whole thing in the first place . . . but it took over two weeks for my back to feel normal again.

The Love Robot has continued to show up at occasional dinners through the years, seeking (demanding) love in the form of hugs to charge its batteries. Ladd hasn't quite warmed up to the Love Robot yet (he says he has a hard time connecting to it on any sort of human level), but I'm going to give it a little more time. The Love Robot has all the patience in the world.

Love Robot Chili and Cornbread Muffins

The Love Robot serves this to her family, and they love it! Season it with dinnertime shenanigans.

LOVE ROBOT CHILI

MAKES 8 SERVINGS

3 pounds ground beef

3 garlic cloves, minced

One 8-ounce can tomato sauce

2 tablespoons tomato paste

1 tablespoon chili powder

1 tablespoon ancho chile powder

2 teaspoons ground cumin

1 teaspoon ground oregano

2 teaspoons kosher salt

¼ teaspoon cayenne

¼ cup masa harina (corn flour)

One 15-ounce can kidney beans, drained and rinsed

One 15-ounce can pinto beans, drained and rinsed

Grated sharp Cheddar, for serving

Sour cream, for serving

Chopped red onion, for serving

Lime wedges, for serving

Cornbread, for serving (optional), such as Green Chile and Cheddar Cornbread Muffins (page 59)

1. Place the ground beef in a large saucepan or Dutch oven and throw in the garlic. Cook over medium heat until browned. Drain off the excess fat, then pour in the tomato sauce, tomato paste, chili powders, cumin, oregano, salt, cayenne, and 1½ cups hot water. Stir together well, cover, and reduce the heat to low.

2. Simmer for 1 hour, stirring occasionally. If the mixture becomes overly dry, add ½ cup water at a time as needed.

3. When the hour is almost up, place the masa harina in a small bowl. Add ½ cup hot water and stir with a fork. Dump the masa mixture into the chili. Stir well, then taste and adjust the seasonings. Add more masa paste and/or water to get the chili to your preferred consistency or to add more corn flavor. Add the beans and simmer for 10 minutes.

4. Serve with grated Cheddar, sour cream, chopped red onion, and lime wedges. Serve with cornbread if you like!

GREEN CHILE AND CHEDDAR CORNBREAD MUFFINS

MAKES 12 MUFFINS

Cooking spray

1⅓ cups yellow cornmeal

⅔ cup all-purpose flour

1 teaspoon kosher salt

1 cup buttermilk

2 large eggs, whisked

2 teaspoons baking powder

1 teaspoon baking soda

1½ cups grated Cheddar

One 4-ounce can chopped green chilies, undrained

6 tablespoons butter, melted, plus softened butter, for serving

1. Preheat the oven to 425°F. Prepare a muffin tin with cooking spray.

2. In a large bowl, combine the cornmeal, flour, and salt.

3. In a small pitcher, combine the buttermilk, eggs, baking powder, and baking soda. Whisk with a fork to combine.

4. Pour the buttermilk mixture into the dry mixture. Stir with a fork until combined. Fold in the cheese, green chilies, and melted butter until just combined.

5. Portion the batter into the prepared muffin tin and bake until a toothpick inserted into the center of a muffin comes out clean, about 15 minutes.

6. Serve warm with softened butter. These go great with chili!

YUM ♡ YUM

Devil Woman

I grew up observing Lent, the forty-day-long Christian season that leads up to Easter. Lent signifies the period of time that Jesus spent fasting (and being tempted by Satan) in the wilderness before his ministry began, and my Episcopalian upbringing taught me that it should be a time of reflection, denial, and sacrifice. I remember as a little girl giving up everything from lemon drops (age seven) to Cheetos (age twelve) to chocolate (ages fifteen, nineteen, twenty-two, twenty-four, and twenty-seven), and now, as an old lady, I still observe Lent by giving up something I really, really like.

In my layman's understanding, I have always believed that the whole point of Lent is to choose something to give up that will cause you daily (several times a day) discomfort or pain. It would make no sense, for example, for me to give up bananas for Lent. I loathe and abhor them, and giving them up would require zero sacrifice on my part. What you want to give up is something you reach for, something you rely on, day in and day out, so that you can, by stopping, remind yourself of Jesus' sacrifice—both in the wilderness and on the cross.

These days, I almost always give up alcohol for Lent, which I realize makes it sound like I am a heavy drinker, which isn't exactly the case . . . but I do enjoy a glass of wine here and there (and here and there and here and there). Giving up chocolate has just become too easy; I've learned over time to skirt the system and satisfy my sweet tooth with gummy bears or crème brûlée. Sugar is always an option, but it appears in almost every food and is difficult to avoid given my food-centric gigs as a cooking show host and bakery owner. Coffee would be at the top of the list of obvious contenders, but I just flat out don't want to give up coffee. It is the first thing I reach for the second my feet hit the floor in the morning, I absolutely need it in order to function, and if I didn't have it, I would be terribly uncomfortable and suffer greatly.

The coffee scenario I have just laid out is the entire point of Lent, and a complete affirmation that if I really want to show off my Christian vigor, I should, in fact, give up coffee. But again—I don't want to. Or to put it a better way: I'm too weak to. Caffeine is a legal stimulant, I'm not breaking any laws by ingesting it, and I'm hopelessly addicted. So for the past decade-plus, during the Lenten season, I have become a teetotaler by giving up all things wine, liquor, and White Claw (I have kids in college). Going without booze for forty days is still a stretch for me—but not the impossible stretch giving up coffee would be.

My husband, unlike me, did not grow up observing Lent. It wasn't taught or emphasized in his small-town Presbyterian church, so it wasn't until he saw me observing the tradition that he decided to jump in, too. Just getting his feet wet, he gave up things like sweets and junk food for the first couple of years. And then, in year three, with all of his typical resolve and breakneck speed, he went straight for the jugular and gave up Dr Pepper.

For context: Ladd has almost zero vices. He does not drink coffee, he does not use any tobacco products, he very rarely drinks beer (let alone any other alcohol), and he has never tried a recreational drug. He may have a little bit of a propensity toward obsessively bingeing Marvel movies, but other than that, he leads a largely addiction-free, habit-free life . . . with one notable exception: Dr Pepper. It is his early morning coffee, his midmorning juice, his afternoon recharge, his evening enjoyment. It is his north, his south, his east and west, to borrow W. H. Auden's phrasing, and I purchase it in bulk along with other household necessities such as toilet paper, lightbulbs, and food.

I actually didn't know Ladd had given up Dr Pepper until about three days into that spring's Lent, mostly because he subscribes to the belief that if you give up something in the name of your faith, you shouldn't call attention to yourself by telling everyone and your neighbor (we don't have neighbors, but still) that you have made this terribly difficult sacrifice. This is biblical—in the book of Matthew, it is spelled out: "When you fast, do not be somber like the hypocrites, for they disfigure their faces to show men they are fasting . . . but when you fast, wash your face so that your fasting will not be obvious to men, but only to your Father." In other words, buck up and put on a happy face, and don't do what Ree does and complain to everyone who will listen that she can't have wine because she gave up all alcohol for Lent. She's a really good Christian girl, after all!

Except with poor Ladd, it was written all over his face that something was wrong, no matter how much he probably willed himself to smile through the pain. A minimum four-Dr-Pepper-a-day habit (usually more) is a lot of caffeine and sugar, and for a large, strong man to go cold turkey one day (all because of a man-made tradition, mind you—not a rule or regulation) is a huge drop off the cliff in energy, mood, and patience. So after seventy-two hours of witnessing my teddy bear slowly metamorphosing into a grizzly with fangs, I pressed Ladd to tell me what was up.

"What the heck?" I said.

He grunted an unintelligible word or two. "Uh buh."

"No, seriously," I continued. "What's the deal?"

He repeated his two-word grunt.

"Honey . . . did someone die? Is the bank taking the ranch?" I asked, just halfway kidding. Only the death of a loved one or the loss of a livelihood could account for such a drastic change of affect and mood. He tried grunting and hissing more vague responses, but finally confided that he'd given up Dr Pepper for Lent and that today, day three, he was struggling.

I responded as any caring, understanding spouse would respond: *"What?!?"* I shrieked, incredulous. *"Have you completely lost your mind?!?"* I was simultaneously relieved that there was an identifiable, objective reason for his rapid spiral downward and irritated that he could be so irresponsible about his Lenten choice. *Dr Pepper? Was he crazy? He couldn't possibly give that up! How would the kids and I survive?* (It was all about us, after all.)

I took a deep breath and gently suggested that perhaps giving up Dr Pepper for forty days when he hadn't gone four days without it since he turned eighteen was a little ambitious and that God would surely understand if he decided to pivot to something a little easier. Like oxygen. He grunted again—something along the lines of "Ugguh mu duh duh uck" which loosely translated to "No, I can do this . . . I just need to get over the hump." Well, said hump took another week to get over, and while he did eventually equalize and do pretty well for the rest of Lent, that week was no picnic. He was draggy, short, listless, sluggish, crabby—and while it required a little marital navigation on my part, mostly I just hated seeing my otherwise energetic, strong, virile, motivated husband go downhill like this. Finally, a few weeks later, Easter morning came, and Ladd celebrated with a chilled can of Dr Pepper, savoring every last drop. I gave thanks to God both for His gift of salvation and for giving me my husband back. I was starting to worry that I'd never see him again.

In the years since, as we approach Ash Wednesday (the day that marks the start of Lent), I become filled with an uncomfortable dread knowing that Ladd will undoubtedly choose Dr Pepper as his sacrifice. It's the one thing that hurts him not to have, and that's all the reason he needs to choose it. Meanwhile I pray in the periphery, not for God to give my husband and me strength to get through it all, but for God to make Ladd give up something else. "Please, God. Let him come to his senses." I even beg Ladd, point blank, not to give it up. "Please, honey," I plead. "*Please*. I will give you one million dollars not to give up Dr Pepper." He laughs at me as if I'm kidding—and I must be kidding, he probably tells himself, because no self-respecting wife who has her husband's best interest at heart would allow herself to be such a stumbling block to his faith by begging him not to make the Lenten sacrifice his heart tells him to make.

He also turned the tables on me last spring, as we were gearing up for our respective forty days. "Hey, I have an idea," he said. "How about you give up coffee? Then we'll both be in the same boat, caffeine-withdrawal-wise."

I couldn't believe he would try to interfere in my faith in such a way! I mean, Lent is between me and God. The nerve of some people.

What Do You Do
with Girls?

I married a man who grew up with two brothers on a male-dominated cattle ranch, and when our first baby was born, it took a few moments before he could grasp that the baby was a girl. So certain had he been that his first (and second, and beyond) child would be a masculine child (to quote Luca Brasi in *The Godfather*) that it was completely evident to me that he hadn't even considered the alternative. We were one of those rare couples in the mid-nineties who didn't find out the gender of our babies before they were born, so it was indeed a complete surprise . . . but in this case, it might have helped soften the shock if he'd found out about it a few months before. His surprise was surprising to *me*, because Ladd had always been very good with numbers. But somehow that whole fifty-fifty gender probability thing hadn't even registered with the poor fella.

Now, I would not in any way suggest that he was disappointed. Our baby Alex was healthy and the birth experience had been a blessed (if slightly messy) moment in our young marriage, so Ladd was first and foremost grateful. But I could tell how much he was trying to process the sharp turn his life had just taken. A firstborn . . . *daughter*? He'd never imagined such a phrase—such a reality—for his future. I studied his face as the nurses cleaned Alex's newborn body and checked her vitals, and for a moment I thought someone might need to check Ladd's vitals, too. I didn't recognize this perplexed look on his face.

My mom and sister came in a few minutes later, and we commenced oohing and aahing over the sweet little nugget in my arms. Since I was preoccupied with the ladies in my life, Ladd wandered out to the waiting room to call his parents and tell them the news. They were out of town (Alex had arrived a week before her due date), and he wanted them to know as soon as possible. After he told his mom the bullet points and she expressed her excitement, there was a long pause on Ladd's end of the line. When Nan pressed him on whether he was okay, Ladd asked his mom a simple, direct question: "What do you do with girls?"

He was being completely forthcoming and honest about what was on his mind and in his heart at that exact moment (a quality that would hold true over the coming years). Ladd was the youngest of three brothers and had spent his childhood working on his dad's ranch and reading Spider-Man comics in his pockets of spare time. His buddies came out to the ranch and fished along the creek, and he poured himself into football and wrestling as he grew older. His siblings were guys, his friends were guys, his college roommates were guys . . . so except for the occasional female cousin or love interest in high school and beyond, he never hung around (let alone lived around) girls or women beyond his mom, whom he did love and admire very much. But let's just say there were no tampons in his bathroom growing up. No perfumed body lotion or lipstick lying around. And definitely no bras on the floor.

I think bras on the floor was exactly what Ladd pictured (and feared) now that he knew he was officially the father of a daughter. Bras on the floor, bras hanging from doorknobs, bras swinging around a ceiling fan, bras under the sofa cushions. Bras everywhere, as far as he knew! Ladd understood how to dwell among guys; he could handle that. He just had zero experience at all in the girl/bra realm. I know this isn't necessarily unusual with many men who've grown up largely around their brothers and friends . . . but in Ladd's case it was highly amplified. As for the ranch, he had no clue how a girl would fit into his world there—saddling horses, wrangling calves, feeding cattle, preg-checking cows, hauling hay, and fixing fence, all of which require a unique level of strength and skill and guts. Could girls even do all that?

When Nan later told me about Ladd's call from the hospital after Alex was born, I asked her how she answered him when he floated his desperate "what-do-you-do-with-girls" query. Her answer was so perfect in its simplicity that I still think about it and try to picture the exchange in my mind: "The same things you do with boys," she told her son.

There's nothing like a mother's advice.

A couple of years later, when I was pregnant with our second baby, both Ladd and I figured it would be a boy and nicely round things out in our household. Ladd's Luca Brasi "masculine child" side had a faded a bit, and when the baby turned out to be a girl, he threw up his hands and completely surrendered to the process. Ladd had both of the girls on horses at a young age, and he took them along with him when he worked on the ranch, showing them the literal and figurative ropes. He bought them little Wranglers, little boots, little Carhartt coats, and little deerskin work gloves.

While it would have been so much easier for him to wake up in the morning and head out the door sans kids, he woke up Alex and Paige and taught them the fine art of getting out of bed before 5:00 a.m. "I don't want 'em to get too used to sleeping in," he explained, fully serious. They were four and two at the time.

The truth is, he loved having the girls with him when he worked on the ranch. They surprised him with their willingness to jump in and do all the things he was doing, even if they were squeamish or scared. The girls were sweet to the cowboys, they loved the animals, and they never minded getting filthy, as evidenced by the condition of their clothes, faces, hands, hair, and nostrils when they got home with Ladd after work. The laundry told quite a story . . . but there was something more, and I could see it in the interaction between the three of them. The girls were tender. Tough when they needed to be, but never afraid to grab Ladd's cheeks with their sweet palms and give him a smooch on the lips, even if he had a hot branding iron in his hand. More than once, after they were tucked into bed and Ladd settled onto the couch for the evening, he'd shake his head, look off in the distance, and say, "Man, I love those girls." He was bitten by the bug, to be sure, and was totally on board for his girl dad role.

So smitten was he that when I finally, at long last,

gave birth to the masculine child he always wanted . . . he didn't even care. Well, he *cared* . . . it's just that gender no longer mattered to him. The same was true when our baby Todd was born a couple years after that. Yeah, they're boys, okay—fine. Yada yada. He was excited for our family to grow, he just didn't care about the boy-girl thing anymore.

Throughout their childhood, even after the boys were old enough to join the cattle working activities, Alex and Paige excelled at ranch work. The boys were fine. "They try hard," Ladd would say with a chuckle. "But *man* . . . those girls are good help." The cowboys confirmed this—especially as the girls moved into their teenage years. Cattle workings on the ranch just went smoother when Alex and Paige were there, as they seemed to know intuitively where to be and what to do, without much direction or instruction. On the ranch, Alex and Paige were essential workers. Suffice to say, they didn't get that from their mother.

When Alex's high school graduation rolled around, both the joy and the pain in the house were palpable. We were a homeschooling family then, and since Alex had attended a co-op in Tulsa, her ceremony consisted of just twelve students who shared the co-op with us. This made the whole event very special, as parents of each student joined them onstage and said a few words about their kid. People were eloquent and composed, and even Ladd and I were both fine . . . until it was our turn to get onstage and begin to speak. I went first, because I've had more public speaking experience than Ladd, but I couldn't get past the first word ("Alex") without choking up. Brave Ladd saved me by taking the mic, and he turned to Alex and spoke from his heart.

He told his oldest child, his firstborn daughter, how proud he was of her—how hard she worked, how kind she is, how much she has meant to him over the past eighteen years. I was sobbing by now, and Alex had tears in her eyes, trying to hold it together. He went on and on, describing her strongest, best qualities and encouraging her to follow her heart and dreams. It was so darn sad, I could hardly stand it. But then, as Ladd was wrapping up his sentiments, I noticed his bottom lip begin to quiver. "Oh, God," I thought, gripping the stage floor with all ten toes. "Please don't let Ladd cry. The world will never be the same."

Ladd Drummond—the cowboy who'd grown up in a male-dominated ranching world—did begin to cry. He cried openly, onstage, in front of a hundred-plus people. He cried because his heart had broken open some eighteen years earlier, when a creature called "girl" had unexpectedly entered his life. And now it was breaking open again. He cried because, like me, he couldn't believe she was moving on to college, and to whatever life had in store for her beyond that. He cried because he would no longer be able to share the bond of the ranch with her on a daily basis.

Which brings me to his line at the end of the graduation speech. "I love you, Alex," he said in almost a whisper. "I think you'd make a top hand on anyone's ranch."

I started crying harder, but I also started laughing, which was a nice excuse to leave the stage immediately. Snot was dripping from my nose and I couldn't see through the tears. It was one of the sweetest, most hilarious, most devastating things I have ever heard . . . and three years later, he did the same thing at Paige's graduation.

God sure gave that cowboy exactly what he needed.

Twenty Interesting Things About Ladd

1. He can't get in bed without taking a shower first.

2. He's never had a sip of coffee.

3. He can feel a crumb in bed from 1993.

4. He can bench three hundred pounds.

5. He's never smoked a cigarette.

6. He went gray at twenty-three.

7. He dated his wrestling coach's daughter in high school.

8. He can't stand lotion.

9. He's scared of the dark.

10. He's never had a glass of wine.

11. He loves movies based on Jane Austen novels.

12. He retains every word he reads.

13. He has an encyclopedic knowledge of the Bible.

14. He likes to watch the boys' football games alone in the press box so he doesn't have to talk to anyone. (He analyzes every play.)

15. He can fall asleep anywhere within five seconds.

16. He has never tried a recreational drug.

17. He loves Spider-Man.

18. He likes to read.

19. He doesn't hunt.

20. He weighs the same as he did in college.

(And Ree!)

1. (I like to shower in the morning.)
2. (I ingest gallons per day.)
3. (I could sleep in a bed of crumbs and never notice.)
4. (I can't do a push-up.)
5. (I smoked Virginia Slims in college.)
6. (I had a gray hair once and plucked it.)
7. (I can't top that.)
8. (I have thirty lotion bottles in my bathroom.)
9. (I long for the dark.)
10. (No comment.)
11. (Me, too!)
12. (I skim and miss 70 percent of the details.)
13. (I only read the parts I like! Ha ha.)
14. (I like to be in the stands with cowbells and orange pom poms screaming and cheering with the other moms! *Go Huskies!!!*)
15. (I have to wind myself down for thirty minutes.)
16. (No comment.)
17. (I love murder documentaries.)
18. (I love murder documentaries.)
19. (Oh deer! Me neither.)
20. *(No comment!)*

Motherhood

Pride, Prejudice, and Epidurals

~

My first childbirth experience went off without a hitch. I began having contractions at home around midnight, then implemented the ironclad procedure I'd drilled on for months: I hopped in the shower, shaved my legs, dried and curled my hair, then put on plenty of makeup and a cute outfit that included a sleeveless denim maternity jacket with embroidered flowers, bless my 1997 heart. Then I woke up Ladd, who'd been clueless about both my contractions and my inappropriately excessive grooming, and we headed to the hospital an hour away. A few hours later, our baby girl Alex was born. Some two years later, Paige, our second child, entered the world without incident . . . albeit not without stitches. (Ow, that smarted.)

I received epidurals with both my baby girls, not because I'd planned to do so ahead of time, but because I had no choice. In fact, I'd never dreamed my body was capable of being overwhelmed by such profound discomfort until I experienced the sensations of labor. It wasn't even pain. Pain is definable and quantifiable, and I actually would have preferred sharp, stabbing pain over the misery I was experiencing. Labor, for me, was an all-encompassing, mind-numbing, total-body level of incomparable suffering that's quite impossible to put into words. It was like I entered "bad cramps" into a Texas Instruments calculator, then multiplied it by one million and pressed the equal sign. My pre-childbirth "Pfft, how bad can it be?" assumptions were very quickly replaced with moans, groans, and, ultimately, panicked pleas to the nursing staff to end the torment and give me anything they had, absolutely anything— or just knock me over the head, whichever would take effect faster. In both of my first two childbirth experiences, once the nurse sat me up and the anesthesiologist inserted that blessed epidural needle into my lower back, I was able to live again and stop regretting the day I ever met Ladd. It was such sweet, sweet relief.

In the months that followed the birth of Paige, it slowly began to gnaw on me that I hadn't been able to resist anesthesia during labor. This was made much worse by the fact that both Hyacinth, my best friend, and Missy, my sister-in-law, had given birth to their babies with no anesthetic assistance at all. *What the heck?* I wondered. What was going on? I was a tall, robust, slightly weird but emotionally stable, moderately tough, bona fide country woman by now—why had I not been able to rise to this challenge? Why couldn't I withstand the pain of labor when centuries—nay, millennia—of birthing mothers had done so before epidurals came along? Why had I caved? I was stumped, defeated, and annoyed . . . and while I was grateful for the good health of my two girls, the navel-gazing side of me needed answers.

I researched and examined all possibilities while the girls took their naps, because it was much more fun than doing laundry. The first internet suggestion I stumbled upon was birth order: Did the fact that I was not a first-born sibling in my family of origin increase my chances of waving the white flag during labor? Great, another middle child issue for me to stew over. A second theory was that women who can't endure the pain of labor and wind up giving in to the relief of anesthesia do so because they are carrying excess emotional pain from their childhood and the cumulative load becomes too much for them to bear. But considering I had grown up eating Cocoa Puffs, watching *Gilligan's Island,* and roller-skating around my neighborhood, I immediately ruled that out. There were yet other suggested factors, from the mother's astrological sign, to the baby's astrological sign, to the barometric pressure at the time of birth. I was about to give up and go throw a load of whites in the washing machine when I saw a new piece of information that immediately piqued my interest.

"Redheads Require Increased Anesthesia," read the headline, and here was the skinny: A new line of scientific thought was emerging that suggested that redheads were of a specific phenotype that seemed resistant to typical levels of pain-numbing meds. A certain mutation that happened thousands of years ago not only caused an absence of pigment in the hair, but also seems to have made us gingers more sensitive to pain. So from dental work to childbirth, redheads were now found to feel pain more acutely and require higher levels of analgesics. This was a revelation. This was *awesome*! Not only was this redhead theory a possible explanation for my utter wimpiness, it also meant, more important, that this whole thing totally wasn't my fault!! I couldn't wait to tell everyone, especially Hyacinth and Missy. Never mind that they had likely spent approximately zero seconds obsessing over the chasm between my labor pain approach and theirs. And while I wasn't certain more babies were in my future, this working theory at least gave me a scapegoat for my past anesthetic failures. It also offered a workable solution for the future, if I were to lose my marbles (or have that second margarita) and get pregnant again: I would simply dye my hair dark brown before my due date!

Just kidding.

Three years later, through a chain of events I'm not going to get into, I did get pregnant again. And while I was plenty busy with my two young daughters, I managed to find time during the third trimester to give myself regular epidural-avoiding pep talks, which of course was much easier than signing up for a Lamaze class, where they taught actual proven methods for avoiding epidurals. But I lived in the country, and the truth is, I guess I didn't like signing up for things. (I still don't.)

In an ironic twist, Hyacinth, my best friend and labor pain nemesis, wound up appointing herself my cheerleader once I confessed my years-long resentment of her dumb, stupid natural childbirth talents. Annoyingly, not only did she not judge me at all for having had epidurals, she told me that every childbirth is different and I shouldn't ever put pressure on myself to have any specific outcome. This infuriated me further. Still, I asked her to *please* be in the delivery room with me when I gave birth this time because I couldn't possibly do it without her. I mean, Ladd was invited, too, and all . . . but I was absolutely resolute. I wanted to give birth without an epidural, and I needed my best friend in order to do it.

Hyacinth, a loyal pal and devout Catholic, took this new responsibility to heart. She gave me, a non-Catholic, a crash course on the Rosary, which, she explained, had been a crucial tool during her births. About two weeks before my due date, after I invited my younger sister, Betsy, to join us in the room as well (I figured the more the merrier at that point!), Hyacinth briefed her, too. My Rosary maidens and I were so excited to bring our child (I mean Ladd's and my child) into the world.

When I went into labor, Ladd and I headed to the hospital with my packed bag and our printed-from-the-internet list of Scottish baby names for both boys and girls. I called Hyacinth and Betsy on the way over and told them Operation No Epidural was officially underway, and before long the four of us were one happy family in the labor and delivery room. Ladd turned on the wall-mounted TV at my request, and we all settled in to watch both the contraction monitor and *One Million Years B.C.*, a prehistoric action-adventure film starring Raquel Welch. It was strangely soothing, and so very odd.

Labor progressed more quickly than expected, and after an hour or two, things started to get uncomfortable. Hyacinth laid her hand on my shoulder and began praying the Rosary, reminding me that this was what we'd been working toward all along and gently reassuring me that I could absolutely do this. The contractions got more intense and started coming more quickly. *Oh, no. Oh, help.* This was stronger than I'd ever felt before. This was getting real. Within minutes, I was writhing and gripping the rails of the hospital bed, trying to do Lamaze breathing like I'd seen it on TV shows. It wasn't working.

I looked up at Ladd, who was standing on the other side of my bed; his jaw muscles were tightly clenched from the stress of seeing his normally mild-mannered wife squiggling around, right on the verge of losing it. I was past the point that either of my previous labors had gone before I buckled, and Ladd was in new territory as well. I glanced over at my sister. She was in the corner of the room, watching through squinted eyes, trying to shield herself from the drama she was witnessing. I looked at Hyacinth in a panic and started making groaning noises that made her so uncomfortable, she yanked the call panel from its holder and slammed her palm on the red button. "We need an epidural in here!!" Hyacinth commanded over the microphone. *"Please hurry!!!!"*

Now that's a good friend right there.

Turns out, I was fully dilated and it was way too late for an epidural. After a few more minutes of hell, I felt an urge to bear down like I'd never experienced in my previous two, anesthetized births. After a few pushes, I let out a primal, piercing, preposterous scream . . . and Bryce (not Hamish or Argyle) was born. I crumpled backward in the bed and draped my arm over my face to shield the uncontrolled tears, which were not from happiness, but sheer relief and exhaustion.

"Hey, it's a boy!" I heard Ladd exclaim. *Oh, that's right—it hadn't even dawned on me to ask.*

"You did it!" Hyacinth cheered. *I'm converting to Catholicism tomorrow.*

"Are . . . you okay?" my little sister whimpered, still backed against the corner of the room. *No way she's having kids after this.*

To this day, while I love all my children equally, I consider Bryce's birth to be my favorite. It made me feel alive, that primal, preposterous scream—I never knew my vocal cords could even produce that sound. And those contractions—I never imagined my body could endure that level of agony. That Raquel Welch film—I got to add an interesting new movie to my repertoire! And the fellowship—I had the pleasure of spending a few hours with three of my favorite people on earth (four, if you count my obstetrician). I did it—I gave birth naturally.

And I didn't have to dye my hair to do it!

Ten More Interesting Things About Redheads

1. Redheads make up 2 percent of the world's population.

2. Redheads make up 13 percent of Scotland's population!

3. I am the only redhead in my house.

4. Redheads don't go gray. They very gradually go straight to white.

5. Red hair is a genetic mutation that likely occurred twenty thousand years ago.

6. Redheads are more sensitive to hot and cold pain. (Not just labor pain!)

7. While redheads are more sensitive to some kinds of pain, they are less sensitive to capsaicin and can therefore tolerate very spicy food. (That explains a lot.)

8. Mark Twain was a redhead.

9. Redheads are said to have a more "robust" love life than other hair colors. I'm just the messenger here . . .

10. Bees are said to be more attracted to redheads because they mistake us for bright flowers. Run!!

Placenta Fail

I didn't mean to get pregnant with Todd. I mean, I guess I know how it technically happened . . . but it was an accident. Well . . . a miscommunication. I won't go into detail. Anyway, when I found out I was expecting him, my fourth baby, I already had two young girls and a nine-month-old baby boy, and because I am a crazy person, I had just started homeschooling. In the wake of the positive pregnancy test, I spent some time on the couch, curled up in a ball, pillow over my face, in both disbelief and dread. How in the world could this have happened?! Oh, that's right . . . I guess I already knew.

Of course, once I got over the shock, it didn't take long for me to fall in love with the burgeoning baby in my womb, and I wound up having a great pregnancy. I was so full of energy, I couldn't see straight! I scrubbed baseboards and the top of my refrigerator, which I would highly recommend, though it's not for the faint of heart. I sorted drawers and gardened as if an apocalypse was nigh. I helped my sister open a ballet studio in our small town. I homeschooled like a champ and felt on top of my game twenty-four hours a day. Four kids? Pfft, no problem. I could do this!

Then one night, five weeks before my due date, I started having contractions.

They started mid-evening and presented themselves as Braxton-Hicks contractions, which happen in the final weeks of pregnancy and are not to be confused with labor itself. But these contractions were a little different, as they never really let up. I tried to ignore them and didn't even say anything to Ladd, and around 10:00 p.m. we headed to bed. By midnight I was still awake, though, and wondering when this bunched-up belly of mine was going to un-bunch.

I finally decided I probably needed to get it checked out. I quietly got dressed, then tapped Ladd on his shoulder to wake him. "Hey, honey," I whispered. "I'm just gonna drive over to the hospital. I'm having some weird contractions and I know it's fine, but I just want to make sure."

Ladd shot up in bed. "I'm sorry, what?" he asked, rubbing his eyes to get them to open.

"I'm gonna drive over to the hospital," I repeated. Mind you, the hospital is an hour from our house. "I'll be back in a little bit; you get some sleep."

"Are you out of your mind?" he asked, grabbing for his jeans. "I'll be ready in two minutes," he said.

"No," I insisted, and reminded him that we had three children under the age of six who were asleep upstairs and that any babysitter or family member wouldn't make it to our house for at least thirty minutes, and I needed to just get over there so I could make sure everything was okay and be back home before morning. "I'm totally fine!" I said. "You stay here and I'll call you when I get there."

He wasn't going to let me drive all the way to the hospital by myself, but he conceded that he couldn't leave the kids at home alone. So here's the harebrained plan we came up with: I would immediately drive to our small town and pick up Brandi, the kids' babysitter. She would then drive me (in my vehicle) halfway to Bartlesville, where the hospital is. At the halfway point on the way to Bartlesville, my dad (who lives there) would meet us. I'd get in his car and he would drive me to the hospital. Meantime, Brandi would turn around and drive my vehicle out to our house on the ranch to stay with the kids so Ladd could *then* drive to the hospital in Bartlesville to be with me. It seemed a little bit like a relay race I participated in when I was on the junior high track team, only this time I was the baton. And the baton had a really huge belly.

I drove to town and met Brandi as planned, we met my dad at the halfway point as planned, and my dad took me to the hospital, where I checked myself in. I told the OB nurses that I was just having some weird contractions, that my due date was still five weeks away and I was sure it was nothing, and that I'd love to head home soon so my husband didn't have to make the drive over. The nurses rolled their eyes, hooked me up to a monitor, and confirmed that I was, in fact, having contractions. But more concerning: my blood pressure was really high, which hadn't been a concern for me in previous pregnancies (or in this one, up until now). Because I was five weeks from my due date, they wanted to try to stop the labor since the baby's lungs wouldn't be quite matured yet, so they gave me a mild medication to try to calm them down. I called Ladd, who had just left the ranch, and gave him an update. It looked like I wouldn't be able to head home anytime soon.

The labor-halting medication didn't work, and the contractions kept on coming. So the medical team tried a second medication, which also didn't work. I really wanted a burger by this point, but apparently burgers aren't permitted when aggressive medications to stop labor are being administered. Finally, at the doctor's orders, the nurses broke out what they called "the big guns," which they said would surely stop the contractions in their tracks. But with this one, they did have a warning for me: "It might make you throw up, sweetie," one nurse said gently, a look of compassion on her face. And boy oh boy, did it ever, just as my handsome husband walked into the hospital room after his hour-long drive. I absolutely did throw up, Linda Blair style, all over the hospital bed, the hospital room, the floor, the monitors, and the world . . . all right in front of Ladd. He tried to act brave, nonchalant, and supportive, but I could tell from the look on his face that he was waiting for my head to spin around. Immediately I noticed that the force of the vomiting had caused my water to break—but instead of clear amniotic fluid all over the bed, it was bright red blood.

I'm sorry to get so graphic, but the point is: I had a placental abruption, which can be extremely dangerous for the baby, so the doctor rushed me to the OR to perform an emergency C-section. The whole thing was all a blur, and I believe they gave me general anesthesia, because I had a lucid dream that my high school boyfriend's cousin (whom I hadn't seen since high school) was touching my belly and telling me how lucky I was that I didn't have any stretch marks after four pregnancies. When I woke up, I discovered that, in fact, my high school boyfriend's cousin was one of the nurses. She really looked great! And how nice of her to notice my stretch-mark-free belly after she had helped pull a child out of a seven-inch incision in my abdomen. This was definitely one of the weirdest nights of my life.

We (somewhat inexplicably) named our baby Daniel, then a few days later changed his name to Todd, after Ladd's late brother. Our Todd had to spend two weeks in the NICU, but everything turned out fine, except for two things. First, after poor Brandi handed me off to my dad earlier in the night and headed back to the ranch, she hit a very large deer on the highway. Ladd found this out when he saw only one headlight working on my Suburban, and a very mangled hood, as Brandi pulled into our homestead. Poor deer! And poor Brandi! (She was fine, thank God . . . albeit slightly freaked out for many weeks.)

Second, the day after the C-section, when the craziness of the previous twenty-four hours had settled down a bit, Ladd was in the hospital room with me as I tried to dig out of my grogginess. "How crazy that I've given birth three times without any issues," I muttered. "And now, on the fourth, I had to have a C-section."

"I'm glad you're okay, honey," Ladd said, looking relieved. I guess it had been a harrowing experience for him, too.

"I don't even really remember the operation," I said. "I just remember you saying that it was a boy." I decided not to go into the whole thing about my high school boyfriend's cousin. Things were already confusing enough.

We talked for a bit about how it had all gone down, and after a few minutes, Ladd smiled and said, "Oh, and guess what?" He grabbed ahold of my toes and wiggled them playfully.

"What?" I asked. I figured he was going to tell me something sweet and romantic to cheer me up and make me feel like a normal wife again.

"Well . . . I saw your guts," he said, an impish grin on his face.

I pushed the nurse button and asked for a strong sedative.

In the years since, I have begged Ladd to tell me that he was kidding, that he stayed north of my shoulders (as I had ordered him to do in all previous births) and on my side of the drape during the whole procedure and had not, in fact, seen the inside of my body. But my beloved husband has never changed his story, and he feels it's important to always tell me the truth. He saw my guts, and no amount of vanity on my part can ever change that.

He does point out that they were the cutest guts he'd ever seen, though. So there's that!

Sword!

⁓

I'd never been happier than I was that morning. My two young girls had stayed with Ladd's parents the night before and were spending the whole day at their house. Ladd had taken our two boys (ages four and two at the time) to work cattle on the ranch with him. I had the whole blessed house to myself for the first time in what felt like seven centuries, and I couldn't wait to settle in, get caught up, and not wipe a single nose (or bottom) for the rest of the day. Free time, for a mother of young children, is the most insanely wonderful delicacy, and I was so hungry for it. The immense glee I experienced when Ladd pulled away from the house with Bryce and Todd was palpable. You know the feeling, maybe it happens a handful of times a year if you're lucky, when you find yourself suddenly awash with extreme happiness and joy—and it feels like everything is 100 percent okay and lovely and wonderful? That was me. I saw nothing but good things ahead. There was hope for my future.

Less than two hours later, however, my phone rang. I saw that it was Ladd, and when I first picked it up, I heard the familiar sounds of ranch work in the background: cows mooing, cowboys hollering, spurs jangling. But there was chaos, too—an unsettling one. I felt it even before Ladd uttered a word. "Todd's burned!!!" he shouted into the phone. I could hear my baby crying—screaming bloody murder, actually. This sounded bad.

My knees instantly turned to spaghetti. My heart not only fell to my stomach, it exited my body and rolled out the door. I felt sick. But then the adrenaline rushed and I kicked into gear. "I'm coming now!!" I shouted, as I started toward the door, wearing whatever I was wearing and shoving my feet into whatever two shoes were most directly in my path. Ladd replied (frantically, for him) that he'd meet me at the highway near the place where they were working so I could scoop up Todd and rush him to the hospital. Every nightmare scenario pummeled my thoughts as I drove ninety miles per hour to our meeting spot.

I was only able to continue breathing during the

drive because Ladd had finally explained on the phone that "Todd's burned!!" meant that Todd had burned his hand. One of the cowboys had set a red-hot branding iron on the ground for a few seconds and Todd spotted it, marveled "Sword!," and picked it up by the hot end. I decided that I would wait until later that evening, after we were all home and bandaged and safe (and bathed), before educating Ladd on the merits of being extremely precise when calling me to inform me that one of our children is sick or injured. "Todd burned his hand," for example, is distressing for a mother to hear, but hundreds of light-years less distressing than "Todd's burned!!!" I couldn't understand how my husband, a man of few words, couldn't have added just two more ("his hand") in order to keep those five years from falling off my life expectancy. I'll never, ever get them back.

Indeed, when I picked up Todd at the highway and quickly inspected his branded palm, I saw that while it probably wasn't a third-degree burn, it most definitely needed medical attention, so we headed to the hospital, which was an hour away. As I began the drive and caught my breath some more, I glanced down and realized that not only had I neglected to change into regular clothes before I bolted out the door, I happened to be wearing the worst possible pajamas in my repertoire:

nine-year-old faded pajama pants with pink flowers, a skimpy orange tank (pink and orange together do not work well on a redhead; trust me), and a moss-green hooded sweatshirt, which belonged to Ladd. The orange tank had been stained with coffee earlier in the morning and since I didn't think I'd see another human being all day long, I hadn't changed it. The pajama pants had a hole in the crotch (I repeat: a hole in the crotch, and a large one), and to make matters worse, I wasn't wearing underwear. Please remember that I'd been home alone. Dressing for success just wasn't on my radar when I woke up that morning.

It was about this time that the burn pain really started to hit Todd and the bloodcurdling (and heart-wrenching) screaming began. It was absolutely awful, and we still had a good forty-five-minute drive ahead. I felt absolutely terrible for him until I caught a glimpse of myself in the rearview mirror as I was checking on Todd—and then I felt absolutely terrible for me as well. No makeup, puffy eyes with yesterday's smudged mascara under them, greasy bangs, mid-thirties pimple. When I say I almost ran off the road because of how unfortunate a sight I was, I am not exaggerating. For a split second I started calculating the time it would take for me to dart by my mother-in-law's house in town in order to change and splash water on my face. But then

Todd let out a real doozy of a wail . . . and I knew I had to put the pedal to the metal and get to the hospital.

Once inside the waiting room of the ER, I nabbed an ice pack for Todd's hand, and it helped his pain immensely. As I held it on his injured palm and stroked his sandy brown hair to comfort him, I was able to allow myself to be temporarily distracted from the shocking state of my own appearance. It also helped when I realized how positively filthy Todd was. He'd been in the cattle pen just long enough that morning to have been covered in all manner of dust, dirt, mud, and manure. And it wasn't just on his clothes; it was on every surface and in every crevice of his body, from his earlobes to his fingernails. His plentiful tears over the previous hour had served only to create a swirly mud painting on his otherwise cherubic face. Todd and I were quite a scary-looking pair.

I understand this might be coming across as false humility: "Oh, I looked, like, *sooooo* bad!" I mean, who really looks that bad in her thirties? But I beg you to trust me on this one. Imagine the worst day you've ever had in your life, attractiveness-wise. Now double that. Now triple that, and add a pair of crotchless floral pajama pants, a coffee-stained shirt, greasy bangs, a zit, and a manure-caked toddler. Then go ahead and triple that again, and that's the sacrilege that was sitting in the waiting room of the emergency room in the town where I'd grown up—the same town where I'd always valued wearing lipstick to match my outfits.

My physician father, already at the hospital seeing some of his own orthopedic patients, dropped by to see us in the waiting room. He did a cursory examination of Todd's hand and affirmed that we'd done the right thing by coming in. Then I caught my dad looking at my clothes and I sensed very clearly that he was quietly wondering where it had all gone wrong with me. My dad would deny this, of course, but you should have seen the way he glanced at my greasy bangs. He couldn't hide his true feelings at all! "I can take it from here, Dad," I insisted. "You have your own patients to see." He was immaculate, and the blue of his creased pants matched the subtle stripe on his perfectly pressed golf shirt. It didn't matter that Todd was clearly comforted by his grandpa being there; I couldn't bear for him to have to hang with us any longer. *No, really, Dad . . . please go.*

The medical treatment Todd received was relatively routine: an application of some kind of super special cream, a great big gauze wrap, and Tylenol with codeine. I kind of wanted to ask for a dose for myself, but since I had to drive all the way back to the ranch, I decided against it. We were discharged, and in a hilarious (sad-hilarious, not funny-hilarious) icing-on-the-cake moment, as Todd and I were walking to the car, I saw the mother of an old boyfriend walking toward the hospital. You seriously can't make any of this up.

She was a good thirty yards away from me, but my red hair tipped her off. "Ree?" the stylish lady said. "Is that you?" That she was looking straight at me and was still not able to discern for sure if it was me is an indication of just how far I'd fallen since my premarital glory days. So I did the only thing I could possibly do in that situation: I feigned a coughing fit, hacking and gagging into my elbow as I walked faster with Todd toward my car. His codeine was kicking in by now and he started giggling at the silly sounds his mama was making, and before I knew it, the old boyfriend's mom had scurried away and darted through the doors of the ER. Anything to get away from me and whatever plague I was infected with.

The ride back to the ranch was uneventful. Todd's pain was under control; he clicked his tongue on the roof of his mouth about a hundred times and said things like, "Mama bom boom beebee" and "Conchy conchy," which made me laugh. Finally, a laugh! I got home, handed Todd to Ladd as I briefly updated him on his baby's medical status, and took an hour-long shower to wash off that whole godforsaken day. When I emerged from the bathroom in clean, non-holey pajamas (I'd sure learned my lesson), I saw that Todd was sound asleep on Ladd's lap . . . with a plastic sword in his hand.

"Funny" Family Injuries on Drummond Ranch

(We're all okay now!)

✳ Todd ran into a barbed-wire fence at full speed. (It was dark outside and he was playing with the dogs. He still has scars!)

✳ I accidentally injected myself with bovine blackleg vaccine. (That's one microbe I don't have to worry about anymore.)

✳ Ladd dislocated his pinkie finger riding his horse. (L.B. bucked and he grabbed the saddle horn too hard.)

✳ Alex stepped on a toothpick and didn't tell me. (It broke off in her heel and turned into an abscess.)

✳ Bryce got a mild concussion. (He fell off his horse!)

✳ I sprained my ankle stepping in a hole. (There used to be a tree there. A tornado had taken it the week before.)

✳ Paige cut her hand on a beer bottle when she was seven. (It wasn't hers. Seven stitches.)

✳ Ladd dropped a two-hundred-pound pipe on my ankle. (He says I dropped it, but it sounds better to say he dropped it. Ouch.)

✳ Todd accidentally injected himself with cattle wormer. (It happens more than you'd think!)

✳ Todd ran past a door and sliced his arm open on a tiny nail sticking out of a board. (Nine stitches.)

✳ Todd singed his face with a flamethrower. (His eyebrows eventually grew back.)

✳ (Todd wins the medal for most mishaps!)

Our Great Homeschooling Experiment

Our first child, Alex, happily attended kindergarten in our small town of Pawhuska, and her first school year was nothing but lovely. Her teacher, Mrs. Reed, taught her about Native American art, language, and culture (not to mention the three Rs), and I had zero complaints . . . except when it came to transportation. Alex had two younger siblings at the time, and in order for me to get her to school in the morning, I'd have to drag all three kids out of bed early, load them all in the car, and haul them to town for the hour-long round trip. Then we'd turn around and make the exact same trip in the afternoon, when it was time to pick her up. After a couple of months of this back-and-forth schlepping, I was already tired of the car and was even more tired of not being able to get much done at home during the day. I'd think about having to feel that way for the next eighteen years (Bryce was just a baby, not to mention the fourth kid, who wasn't even a twinkle in my eye yet), and I felt overwhelmed.

So I decided to give the ol' school bus a try; I was surprised to learn that it actually did pick up country kids! The only problem was that our ranch was the farthest away from town, so we had to be the first stop on the morning route. This meant the driver would pick up little five-year-old Alex at 6:45 a.m., and she'd ride along on the rest of the rural stops, finally making it to school by 8:15—an hour and a half on the bus for my little pookie head. In the afternoon, the reverse was true: She was last to be dropped off, usually as late as 4:30 p.m. I always felt sorry for Alex when I went outside to meet the bus; she was usually passed out, her soft cheek smudged against the window of the bus. The school bus obviously wasn't turning out to be ideal, so that whole year we toggled between the two ride options, with Ladd jumping in and helping when he wasn't on his horse. (Though honestly, the horse might have taken less time.)

Summer came, and we so enjoyed not having to fight the whole transportation thing. Around that time, my best friend, Hyacinth, and I had dinner with some couples from Tulsa. We were picking their brains about ideas for an art camp we were thinking of organizing, and we'd never met them before that night. They were all exceedingly hip, very intelligent, really funny, and they were spiffy to boot. During the course of our art camp conversation, one person in the group casually mentioned that they all happened to be . . . home-schoolers. I did a double take. I asked the person to repeat himself. I was shocked and confused. I couldn't square it! Homeschoolers? It didn't seem possible.

Hyacinth and I prodded, and as the parents de-scribed their reasons for homeschooling and their ap-proach to education, I studied each of them. These people did not fit the stereotype of "homeschooler" I had somehow formed in my head. For example, I didn't know homeschoolers drank wine! How cool was this? Hyacinth, whose daughter, Meg, had also just finished kindergarten, looked at me after our discussion and we whispered to each other, almost in unison, "Should we do that?" Not once had I even remotely considered homeschooling before, but that night I lay awake in bed and mulled over the new world of possibilities.

I mentioned it to Ladd in passing the next day, imag-ining he'd laugh and tell me I was crazy for consider-ing it. Instead, he said immediately, "I think it sounds great—let's do it!" He'd seen firsthand the difficulty of Alex's transportation to and from school the whole previous school year, and with (then) three kids, he saw how untenable it could become. And if you think he wasn't also calculating how much more ranch help he could get out of this . . . well, ha ha. Ranchers are always thinking about ways they can find more help.

After a couple of weeks of intensive research, I was 100 percent on board the homeschooling train, and we dove in that fall. I bought a globe, a chalkboard, and an abacus. I followed the classical education approach of studying one era of history for an entire school year, and we started with the ancients. We got together with Hyacinth and her kids for a co-op day once a week. One day we had a Roman lunch and put our baby boys in matching togas. That Halloween, the girls and I dressed up as a Cleopatra trio, because by golly, we were home educators now, and every single experience, no matter how ordinary, was a chance to learn about the world. We sang songs about Mesopotamia and the Roman Empire, and Alex memorized a new Greek and Latin root every day. It was a time of exciting new discovery, and I marveled on a daily basis at the comprehensive first-grade education I was receiving! (Oh, and Alex, too.)

This period of time was also what I now refer to as the "acquiring phase" of homeschooling: If there was a workbook, reference book, set of math manipulatives, life-size skeleton, or wall-sized mural, I bought it. I went toe to toe with a fellow homeschooler on eBay over an out-of-print visual reference of the ancient world. (I lost, and I don't think I've ever quite gotten over it.) A storage closet in our home that my mother-in-law had once used for sporting equipment and out-of-season clothes was soon overrun with maps, markers, file folders, and other supplies. I decided I wouldn't be content until our house was its own Staples location.

That first two or three months of homeschooling, I followed an extremely rigid schedule—and I completely set myself up for failure. I thought if I meticulously scheduled every thirty-minute time slot during the day, Alex and I would stick with a game plan and we'd get everything done. But then Paige would need something. And then Bryce would cry. Then Ladd would come home. Then the cows would knock down the fence and get in the yard. Then the dogs would get sprayed by a skunk. And the domino effect would cause our homeschooling schedule to come crumbling to the ground, day after day after day.

Then one dark and stormy afternoon, I found out I was pregnant again. *How could this have happened?!?* That item wasn't in one of the preplanned time slots! (Also, nausea and science experiments are not a good combination.)

At some point during that first year, Hyacinth and I decided, for the sake of our long-term friendship, that we did not have compatible homeschooling styles *at all*, and we needed to suspend our co-op days for the time being. She was very much a type A homeschooler in all the positive ways, with a start and end time for each day (and each subject). She had worksheets printed the night before, and put bookmarks in place so they'd know what they had to get done. Hyacinth had so much discipline and sense of purpose, she'd never dream of throwing up her hands and calling it a day before the work was done; I did it a minimum of once a week. She'd been so kind and generous to bring her kids out to my house every Thursday to do some "shared learning" together, but sometimes she'd arrive and we'd still be looking for underwear, and I think she realized she was better off blazing forward at her own house.

So it was then that I decided not to fight, but to embrace, my haphazard, irresponsible nature and not try to be something I wasn't. Where Hyacinth was a type A home educator, I was more of a type L. I assigned myself the title of "relaxed homeschooler," and there was no looking back. I'd wake up with a rough sense of what our educational objectives looked like that day and I'd shoot for a general start time . . . but sometimes we'd start an hour later. Sometimes two. We'd have spelling tests in the bathtub and drill on math problems while I folded laundry. Some days we'd forget to do math altogether. (Sorry, Alex.) We sang memory songs and made a lot of jam. I hardly ever used the chalkboard, except to leave Ladd little love notes for him to see on his way out the door in the morning. If I felt a subject was above my pay grade, I'd buy a DVD series and park Alex in front of it while I made Paige a snack or gave Bryce a bath. It worked for us! For a while.

When it came time for Paige to start school, it was a little bumpy trying to navigate two different grade levels, but I somehow managed to hold it together most days. Unfortunately, Paige liked to do crafts, and I'd never owned a glue gun before (see page 136). She liked to wear an old Richard Nixon mask while practicing cursive; it was a costume I'd worn in college years earlier, and this really confused Ladd. As a check and balance, I'd take the girls for standardized tests every couple of years to make sure I wasn't messing them up too badly. I never got to the bottom of whether their less-than-impressive math scores were due to nature (math isn't my strong suit) or nurture (therefore, I was never enthusiastic about teaching it), but by and large they were doing fine from an educational standpoint.

An unexpected benefit started showing itself, too. The girls got to take part in life on the ranch a lot more than if they were away at school during the day. If Ladd needed help sorting cattle at the pens, he'd borrow Alex for thirty minutes here or there. If he was shorthanded, he'd take Paige to gather cows. It was then that I realized my "relaxed homeschooler" approach had to have been divinely inspired, as it would have been a tough game of tug-of-war if I felt Ladd was interrupting my schedule to take the kids to work with him. As it so happened, I had no schedule! So marital harmony could continue on—and besides that, the kids were receiving a lot of agricultural education as a bonus course.

My mind would sometimes wander during those long school days. I once conceived of a T-shirt line I would market only to homeschoolers (talk about a sound retirement plan!) with sayings that were plays on old slogans:

"Homeschooling . . . because they're worth it" hinted at the old L'Oréal ads.

"My homeschooler can beat up your honors student." I must have been under stress that week.

My favorite idea of all time was a nod to Porsche in the eighties: "Homeschooling: There is no substitute." (Get it?)

But then I'd veer off course and occasionally come up with more inappropriate ideas: "Homeschooling parents do it on the kitchen table" was one. I guess I was slowly losing my good sense.

It's worth mentioning that I never actually manufactured any of these T-shirts. They were just passing ideas swirling around in my scattered brain along with Latin roots, fractions, and eBay curricula auctions. My days were packed and busy. And once the boys hit their schooling years, all bets were off. It was too much for me to keep track of, and there was an unfortunate incident with Bryce wherein he asked me at age nine what a nickel looked like. (Seems I'd forgotten to cover the currency lesson in our early math program. Oops.) Also, I noticed that sometimes the confines of homeschooling would wear on my nerves. Toward the end of summer, a Staples commercial would come on TV and show a dad happily dancing through the aisles buying school supplies while "It's the Most Wonderful Time of the Year" played in the background. I remember actually telling the nice dad to "shut up" before turning off the television. I never got to experience that same glee every fall.

Over the next several years, I would adapt our homeschooling approach to what our family (and the kids) needed. The girls started attending a classical co-op in Tulsa, which really took their schooling to another level. I kept homeschooling the boys for a time, then tried the co-op, but it wasn't a fit for their wild, unruly, pee-outside natures. Besides, as I was driving them to Tulsa the first few times, it occurred to me that this whole driving and living-in-the-car thing was the whole reason we'd tried homeschooling to begin with, and here I was again. Bryce and Todd ultimately wound up at public school in Pawhuska so they could play football—and it's been a great decision for them. Go, Huskies!

Knowing what I know now, I would absolutely choose to homeschool the kids again. They got to spend a lot of their earlier years together most of the time, and they got to be more a part of ranch life than if they'd gone to public school from day one. I got to enjoy them at home for more of their childhoods, and while I haven't done a scientific poll, I'd guess that most of the kids are glad for their homeschooling experiences. At least that's what they say when I ask them to their face . . . with a twenty-dollar bill in my hand. (Just kidding.)

I have to say that I wouldn't mind the opportunity to go back and teach Bryce that currency lesson. It still comes back to bite him sometimes! (Nickels can be very confusing.)

Adventures in Children's Time

I could write an entire book about the myriad times Ladd has pushed, pulled, encouraged, nudged, or prodded me to do something that I otherwise would never have chosen to do if left to my own devices. I am very comfortable right where I am, thank you very much, and he knows that if he doesn't occasionally light a fire under me, I'll just stay in my delicious comfort zone forever, happy not to have to mess with or factor in anything new. Ladd is my husband, but he's also a human match in that regard. (Blowtorch is more like it.)

Ladd and I tried our hand at an evangelical church for the first two years of our marriage, but we would eventually put down our roots at First Presbyterian Church and have been worshippin' and tithin' and fellowshippin' there ever since. The congregation is comprised mostly of ridiculously sweet retired people who've lived in Pawhuska their whole lives, and we were the youngest family there (by far) for quite a few years. Like most small churches, ours relies on the support and participation of congregants when it comes to the various aspects of carrying out a Sunday service, and our pastors through the years have always encouraged members to volunteer to be lay readers, greeters, and the like. I never sign up for anything, because I just want to go to church, be blessed, have a cookie and a mug of punch, then go straight home, where my comfort zone is waiting to welcome me with open arms and a soft pillow. But I'm always grateful for the kind souls who throw their hat in the ring and help out.

During one Sunday service when the kids were all young, our minister at the time, Pastor Judy, exhorted those of us in attendance to please consider jotting down our names on one of the sign-up sheets after church. There hadn't been many joiners lately, she explained, and she just wanted to reiterate how much she'd love for others to jump in and help. Of course, "others," to me, meant "everyone *but* me," so after the blessing and benediction, I walked right past the sign-up sheets and straight out the white double doors of the church without even glancing in the direction of the bulletin board.

There were no cookies that Sunday, and I needed to get home and make lunch (and cookies!). I couldn't get on my way fast enough.

Over our BLTs at home a little later, Ladd dropped a bomb on me. "Oh," he said, as if it was just a frivolous afterthought, "I signed you up for children's time."

Funny, Ladd. "Ha ha," I responded. "Right." Obviously, he was kidding, as he would never do that to someone he loved.

"No, I really did," he said. "You're signed up for four Sundays in a row starting next week." He took a big bite of his sandwich and grinned. He wasn't kidding after all.

"You . . . *what?*" I said. My cheeks immediately turned hot.

I should take a moment to explain children's time for those of you who have not attended a mainline Protestant church in the last seventy-five years. In many Methodist, Disciples of Christ, and Presbyterian church services, ministers will welcome the younger children to the front of the church for a few short minutes, where they will chat with the kids, ask them thought-provoking questions, and ultimately impart an easy-to-comprehend lesson about life and faith. It's not a children's sermon (it's more interactive than that), and it's certainly not a craft or activity (responsible ministers don't allow glitter in the sanctuary)—it's just, as the name suggests, time with the children, before the real meat of the service (prayer of confession, the sermon, and communion) happens. In recent years, the various pastors at our church had started inviting parishioners to assume the children's time role, but there hadn't been many takers. Seems children's time was at the bottom of the list of things any adult in our church wanted to do.

I, for one, had certainly never volunteered to do it. This was well before I'd started blogging, let alone published any books or done speaking engagements. I was terrified of public speaking to the point of it being a phobia, having had a couple of uncomfortable experiences in both junior high speech class (I said "a whole nother" and heard snickers in the back) and a friend's wedding (I lost my place in the scripture, then said "amen" in a panic and quit), and if I never got up and spoke in front of a crowd the rest of my life, I would be so happy. And that's what's so daunting about doing children's time in church: You're speaking directly to a group of little kids, but you're also doing it in front of the whole dang church. So you have two intimidating audiences to face.

"Well, our kids make up most of the crowd, anyway," Ladd continued. "And I thought you'd be really good at it." *Oh, nice try, honey. The ol' flattery trick won't work for you this time!*

But it did work. In the spirit of Martin Luther, I protested and protested again, but I could tell Ladd really wanted me to try it, and besides that, my name was already on the sign-up sheet. In order to renege, I would have had to call the church secretary the next morning and say, "Never mind, take my name off the list," or worse, break into the church in the middle of the night and scrawl out my name with a black Sharpie. Back then, a local paper was regularly publishing mug shots from the town's weekly arrests, and I really wanted to avoid making an appearance in that column if I could help it. I was trapped.

The following Sunday, with my nervous system in high gear, I walked slowly to the front of the church, ten minutes after the church service began. It was time . . . for my first children's time. At Pastor Judy's invitation, the kids in the congregation—my four, plus three others—walked, crawled, skipped, stumbled, somersaulted, and/or sprinted to the front of the church. "Hey, kids!" I said nervously, as we all sat down on the steps that led up to the altar. As for my message, short of having anything brilliant to say myself, I had tracked down a lesson called the "Five Finger Prayer," a commonly used, nifty tool designed to teach children how to remember the different kinds of people they can pray for.

My heart pounded and my voice shook as I explained the concept of the prayer hand, pointing to each trembling finger as I explained: The thumb is closest to us, and reminds us to pray for our family and friends. The pointing finger tells us to pray for those who instruct and point us in the right direction: our teachers, coaches, and ministers. The middle finger is the tallest, I told them, and prompts us to pray for our president and other leaders. The ring finger is our weakest finger, I explained, and should remind us to pray for those who are sick, sad, hurting, or oppressed. And finally, our little finger represents ourselves, in the vein of "The least of these shall be the greatest among you." If we routinely pray for others first, I told the kiddos, we are more equipped to pray for ourselves. The message was wrapping up and I was still a nervous wreck, but by some miracle, I'd gotten through it in one piece. I glanced at Ladd in his pew and he gave me a sexy wink, which he really shouldn't do in church. But it did make me feel more at ease.

My message drew to a close and I held hands with the kids and said a short prayer, which is customary. Then, just as I was about to make a clean getaway, five-year-old Alex raised her hand out of the blue.

"Yes, Alex?" I said, just as a teacher would call on her pupil.

"You should never, ever, ever do *this*!" she loudly announced, shooting her middle finger straight up in the air, basically giving me the bird in front of everyone. A couple of people in church laughed. A couple more chuckled in an "isn't that cute" way. But most were dead silent. Please don't ever be silent if a young child flips off her mother in front of everyone during children's time. Please laugh, or start singing . . . or something. That poor mom needs your support.

That kicked off what has now been about eighteen years of my doing children's time in our little Presbyterian church, all because my husband signed me up one Sunday when the kids were small. There were some pretty rocky moments in that first year: One time I accidentally attached the clip-on microphone to my shirt with the tip facing in against my skin instead of out. So rather than amplify my voice, it amplified my nervous, pounding heartbeat. Ladd told me he was actually worried about me and almost called 911.

Then there was the little girl who shouted "Jesus!" in answer to every question I asked:

"So, kids . . . what do you think of when you think of God?"

"Jesus!" the little girl replied. Okay, that worked.

"Hey, kids . . . what's more important: being right? Or being nice?"

"Jesus!" Hmm. Well, if you believe Jesus is the answer, I guess she has a point.

"Hey kids . . . who are you cheering for in the Super Bowl: Patriots or Giants?"

"Jesus!" No, sweetie. You have to pick a team.

"I have a question, kids: What's your favorite dessert in the whole wide world?"

"Jesus!" Um . . .

Bless her. I guess she was working on probabilities. Jesus worked in about 40 percent of the questions I asked, so it was probably a great approach.

There were restless boys, shrieking toddlers, kids who were too shy to speak, kids who wouldn't stop talking, and lots of awkward moments that made me cringe. But overall, I'm so glad Ladd kicked me out of my comfort zone and shoved me into the world of children's time. It's kept me from being too lazy at church, and in a nice twist, I can see where it set the stage for my being able to survive the speaking engagements that lay in my future. (If I can survive an audience of little kids, I can survive an auditorium of women!) I usually try to come up with fun messages for children's time, ones that wind up giving the congregation something to think about as well, and they're often peppered with pop culture references that appeal to both my and the older members' generations. (I told the kids all about Elvis Presley once, and a couple of older ladies hooted and hollered in the back.)

Best of all, my daughter Alex holds the record of being the only child who ever gave someone the finger inside our Presbyterian church.

Amen.

Scaring (and Scarring) the Kids

When I was little, my two biggest fears were earthquakes and sharks. This was a bit of a head-scratcher considering I grew up in landlocked Oklahoma . . . but a child's fears aren't always based in logic. It's also puzzling that given these fears, I wound up choosing to go to college in Southern California, where both sharks and (especially) earthquakes were more likely to be encountered. But I'm a mystery in that regard.

When my children were little, however, one of my biggest fears was that they would be kidnapped. This was somewhat understandable given something that happened to me years earlier: In my senior year of high school, I was robbed at gunpoint while exiting my ballet studio late one night. The group of six men got away with my car after I (miraculously) managed to break loose and run to safety, and I was lucky to have been physically unharmed. The perpetrators were apprehended a few days later after tragically murdering a woman who was out walking her dog (my car had broken down on the dirt road where she was walking), and they were convicted and sent to prison. This trauma was obviously a life-changing experience, and it caused me to feel simultaneously grateful, guilty, grieved, and guarded. Add to this a habit of consuming true crime books in those formative years, and I hit my twenties convinced that danger lurked behind every bush, around every corner—and the only way to keep oneself from being a victim was to be hyperaware and vigilant.

And so, once I had my daughters, I found I was largely unafraid of illness or disease; kidnapping was all I thought about. Most medical conditions had a treatment or a cure, I reasoned, and since I'd grown up with a physician father, I was confident that I'd be able to spot symptoms that might spell trouble and get my kids the assistance they needed. I wasn't overly scared of accidents, either—I didn't worry about the tiny girls riding huge horses or them going along with Ladd when he worked with (and sometimes wrestled) eight-hundred-pound animals. He'd grown up on the ranch, after all, and had come through in one piece—

and besides that, I figured that most accidents that happen on a ranch were probably minor, and nothing a splint, a cast, or stitches couldn't fix. I could wrap my head around microbes and medicine, around splints and stitches.

But kidnapping? I simply couldn't bear the thought, and given my brush with criminals during my formative years, I felt more vulnerable to this kind of scenario and wanted to make sure it never, ever happened. Also, living on an isolated cattle ranch, my kidnapping fears were allowed to deepen, fester, and mutate, because it was (in my mind, anyway) such a kidnap-free zone out there, which in contrast made town feel like a more dangerous place. Whenever the girls and I did go out to public places, I was glued to them, squeezing their hands too tightly and carrying them on my hip even if it made my shoulders hurt. I was utterly convinced that stranger danger existed all around us (never mind the fact that stranger abduction is statistically rare) and that I was the only thing keeping the bad element away. When the girls got big enough to go on outings with my mom or mother-in-law, I drilled them on never walking away from their grandmothers in a public place . . . and I used a Sharpie to scrawl my name and phone number on the bottom of their bare feet, just in case they became separated. I gave no thought as to whether this was normal behavior; I just knew it felt necessary. Lord knows where I had even learned that trick.

When the girls got a little older and Alex started kindergarten, I began taking them to Miss Laura's Day Care two days a week in order to have a few hours at home with baby Bryce and to hopefully get some dang housework done. Work and catching up was the plan, anyway—but to get to Miss Laura's house after kindergarten, Alex rode the school bus, and when I realized the bus stop was three houses down, my mind went crazy over the possibilities of all that could go wrong. So I started driving to town early so I could secretly park across the street and make sure Alex made it from the bus to Miss Laura's, then I'd just kill time in town for a couple of hours until it was time to pick them both up. Never mind that this completely negated the benefit of my sending the girls to day care in the first place. At least they never got kidnapped!

My second fear during those years of motherhood was the enormous pond behind our house, which was actually more of a legitimate danger. Drowning, after all, is a serious threat to children, and our pond—which is about twenty-five yards behind our house—was a constant source of terror for me. It's a large water source for cattle, and any kind of security fence or pool-type barrier isn't possible—so it was just about keeping the kids away from it until they learned to swim. This was relatively simple when I just had my two girls: They loved to stay in the house, play with toys, and watch *Teletubbies*, and I could easily be outside and watch them anytime they wanted to go play. I cautioned them regularly about the dangers of the pond, and a simple "no" kept them far away. Ah, they were so cute and compliant.

Then I had two boys, and the little hooligans never once sat down. They wouldn't watch TV. They wanted to be outside all the time, especially Bryce, so just in case I might have my eye elsewhere or they slipped out the door without my knowing, I decided to start putting the fear of God in them regarding the pond. I'd pull up pictures of great white sharks on the internet, preferably ones with blood from a fresh kill all over their teeth. "Sharks! Pond!" I'd say, pointing behind our house. I'd find videos of a congregation of alligators attacking their prey, splashing and chomping in disorder and chaos. "Alligators! Pond!" I'd say, and I'd point out back again. But the most effective was our unit on piranhas. Images of their razor-sharp teeth made Bryce's eyes grow enormous, and he would walk around the house saying, "Bad fish! Pond! Bad fish!" My (truly evil, based on nothing but lies) parenting plan was working.

At this time, Todd was still basically a baby and on my hip twenty-four hours a day, so I didn't worry much about him. The girls had received swimming lessons and were competent swimmers. And Bryce was now suddenly so terrified of the pond that he wouldn't let himself get within fifty feet of it. He was actually scared of the word "pond." And I was confident I'd laid an effective foundation with Todd as well. For the first time since I became a mother, I felt like I'd earned my keep. That dumb pond was no longer an albatross around my neck. My work here was done!

I'd done such a good job, in fact, that Bryce became scared of the bathtub and switched to showers (a sharp contrast to my switching away from showers after watching *Psycho* in sixth grade, but that's another story for another time). He refused to take swimming lessons when my mother-in-law took him to the swim school that summer—and by "refused," I mean he screamed bloody murder when he saw the pool, and he almost *committed* murder when the swim instructor tried to lower him into the water. He thrashed and splashed about so wildly that they almost had to refill the pool when he and my mother-in-law left. Nan's poor face was shell-shocked when she delivered him back to the house that day. Yes, I—mother of the year—had ensured that my sweet, happy firstborn son now suffered from a wicked fear of water, and he wouldn't voluntarily get into a swimming pool until he was about ten. He still refuses to watch *Jaws*.

Over the next several years, we had our share of mishaps and injuries where the kids were concerned. They also had some high fevers, flus, and infections. But thankfully, they came through unscathed . . . and never once fell into the pond or got kidnapped.

As for Alex and Paige, they still have strong memories of how much it tickled when I wrote my phone number on their feet. "Mom, you had issues," they like to say. (Pfft. They have no idea.) But they do concede that my crazy protectiveness taught them to be extra mindful when they left for college, and they seem to think it served them well even though they still give me grief about it.

As for Bryce, he's still not a big water person. He chose the path of football, which takes place squarely on land, lucky for him. He's never going to want to live at a lake, that's for sure.

As for my own childhood fears, I experienced a 6.8

earthquake my freshman year at USC and lived to tell about it. I'm never in the ocean, so I don't see sharks showing up in my life anytime soon.

Today, as a "normal" mother, I still fear for my kids' safety, but I'm able to keep it reined in. I just wake up, say, "Jesus, take the wheel" (thank you, Carrie Underwood), and go on about my day.

I still have a drawer full of Sharpies, though, for when my grandchildren come along.

Wrong Mother

P aige is one of my two middle children, and she and
I have a strange but beautiful relationship. While
my oldest, Alex, will always have the piece of my heart
that can be occupied only by a mother's firstborn child,
Paige is a part of my soul in a way that's hard to explain. And while it's only natural for a mother whose
kids are getting older to look back on the things she
could have done better, I'm a little harder on myself
when it comes to the job I did with Paige. She would
deny and disagree with this: I can't help but feel like
she got the wrong mother in some ways.

Paige, of all my kids, was the most physically attached to me, starting when she was a newborn. For
one thing, she wound up in our bed every single night
during the breastfeeding months. I tried to be disci-

plined, as I'd been when Alex was a baby, and put her back in her crib after the middle-of-the-night feedings. But when Paige woke up crying, I was so exhausted (second child and all) that I just took her back to bed with me, hooked her on, and fell back into a deep sleep. This went on for months, so we had plenty of Paigie/Mama time. For another thing, she was just a squishy and delicious child, with fat Michelin baby legs and the sweetest nose-crinkling, toothless grin. Where I'd been a cautious new mother with Alex and had handled her more delicately and purposefully, I couldn't get enough of baby Paige and was constantly sniffing her head, squeezing her thunder thighs, and eating her up.

Of all the kids, Paige had the hardest time being away from me as a young child. When I had to stay in the hospital with Todd for the first couple of weeks following his birth, Paige felt my physical absence and plastered herself to me during our brief visits. If I'd had a pouch, she would have gladly crawled inside of it and lived there. During her early elementary years, she'd hug me and exclaim, "I love you so much," with so much emotion that I felt it rather than heard it. Ladd noticed and often remarked about Paige's palpable connection to me, and while I was absolutely loath to concede that I had any deeper feelings for her than for Alex and the boys, I always felt the bond, too. She was my sweet Paigie girl. I'm crying as I write this! Waaahhhh.

As Paige got older and moved into her preteen and teenage years, we remained close . . . but things between us grew more complicated, as often happens between mothers and daughters (right, Mom?). For one thing, Paige grew very tall (over six feet) . . . and she developed a personality to match her towering height. She was (and is) very strong, very headstrong, completely self-aware, and pretty much always certain of what she wants and how she feels. Basically I'm trying to say the word "bossy" without saying the word, which I just did—but actually, "bossy" doesn't do Paige justice. She's complex and layered, with a very soft underbelly and an even softer heart. Just don't even think about crossing her. (I'm only halfway kidding.)

I actually love that Paige is this way, because I don't worry about her like I did when she was young. Today she wouldn't think twice about taking out anyone that posed a danger to her (or anyone she loves), and she could probably throw most average humans on the ground in a headlock within two minutes. So there's that. But also, when I think about relationships that might happen in Paige's future, I feel so good knowing she'll always be willing to be completely forthcoming with her feelings, concerns, complaints, and expectations. She won't be a pushover, and whoever her life partner turns out to be, they won't ever wonder where they stand with her.

So back to me being the wrong kind of mom for Paige. Again, she would never agree that I was anything but the right mom, and she is clear in her love and regard for me. Unless I've ticked her off about something, which happens regularly. However, there were four major ways I know I fell short for her during her adolescence, not because of what I did, but who I was. (And, most notably, who I wasn't.)

First, I was not a crafty mother. While I made feeble attempts to occupy the girls' time with arts and crafts projects (which I probably purchased in the form of beginner boxed kits from Hobby Lobby) when they were little, I've always been much more comfortable in the kitchen, and in high school, when we had the choice of taking cooking or sewing class, I always chose the food route. I'm Ree Drummond, and I've never used a sewing machine. I do not own a glue gun. I can hardly sew on a button. For reasons I don't fully understand, the thought of having a closet full of tempera paint, scissors, and beads makes me feel like bursting into tears and running away. And while Alex couldn't have cared less about crafting, I could sense that Paige was always looking in drawers and rummaging through closets, wondering where the glitter—the glitter that all good moms have—was being kept. This became even more difficult in junior high, once the girls started attending a homeschooling co-op in the city. Paige became friends with some of the other homeschooling children, but only the ones whose moms had dedicated craft rooms in their homes. One mom had a dedicated craft *floor* in her home, with separate rooms for sewing, painting, and scrapbooking. Paige didn't understand how this whole aspect of her childhood had gone so wrong.

Second, I was a tardy mother. All the time. To everything. I have wrestled with this over the years, I'm not proud of it, I've tried to shame myself into getting better, and I'm trying to change this very fundamental flaw in myself. I'm late to church, for goodness sake. Alex never really cared; she's cut from the same cloth as me, and didn't complain (or even mention) when I made her late to soccer practice, co-op, Sunday school, or birthday parties. Thank you, Alex! You're the greatest. But for Paige, this was all completely inexcusable and unforgivable. For her not to be ten (fifteen is better) minutes early to everything—and, in fact, to be late to many things—was a cause of great stress to her as a young teenager. After enough late episodes, until she got her driver's license, she started asking Ladd (who's also routinely ten to fifteen minutes early for everything) to drive her places instead. I'll bet they spent all their time in the car talking smack about me and my lateness. Haters!

Third, on a more superficial level, I did not dress like the other mothers. After a few years of my showing up to her soccer and volleyball games (and homeschool co-op days) wearing some variation of a loose, flowy, floral shirt, dangly earrings, and skinny jeans, Paige asked me a simple question one day:

"Mom, can you just wear a T-shirt and shorts sometimes?" she asked.

"No," I answered.

"No?" she responded.

"No," I repeated.

The reason I answered no is that I don't own a pair of shorts, because I'm a redhead and my legs aren't tan. And I don't own any T-shirts because they're short sleeved and I don't like my elbows. But I didn't want to go into these details, because God forbid I pass any of my body-related hang-ups on to my impressionable adolescent daughter. So "no" seemed like a much more fruitful response. Now, I did compromise at a certain point and I tried to choose cotton or gauze for their games and leave the silk-rayon blends just for my cooking show . . . but everything—absolutely everything—

was floral. Poor Paige. I've ruined her on flowers forever. When she has her own flower garden someday, she's probably going to plant nothing but craggy, prickly cacti. Or just fill it with rocks.

Finally, and this is a fundamental difference between Paige and me, I'm not a mother who likes to go do things. The best example of this is when I took Paige and Alex to New York on a work trip. We had reservations in a nice hotel and after the two-leg flight from Tulsa, I was ready to plop down on one of the double beds in our fluffy, posh room and relax. Alex, again, is my clone in this regard, and at fifteen, she was content to crawl under the covers with me and watch *Forensic Files* for the next three hours, then get in our pajamas and order room service. But Paige had other expectations.

"What . . . are you doing?!" she demanded, completely incredulous that I was horizontal in Manhattan.

"What do you mean?" I asked, playing dumb and snuggling deeper into my covers.

"Mom, please get up!" she commanded. "We have to go!"

Go? Go where? I didn't have any work responsibilities until the next day. "Oh, c'mon—let's just veg!" I said. Alex nodded and agreed with me, which made things worse.

Paige looked at the clock, exasperated. "We've got to be at the Statue of Liberty by two in order to get back in time for dinner, so we can make it to Magnolia Bakery before they close, because tomorrow we won't have time! And we have to go to the LEGO store tomorrow before your meeting, then get tickets to Top of the Rock and go take the carriage ride in Central Park!" This is how Paige's mind works. We hadn't even been in New York an hour, but she could see the clock ticking away and all her plans disintegrating with each passing minute. All I could think about was getting the most out of the money I was spending on that hotel room. The rest of the trip was defined by my pulling Paige toward my cocoon and Paige pulling me out into the world. The same tug-of-war still happens today.

I brought all of this up to Paige in passing lately, telling her (somewhat in jest, but also as a confession) how sorry I am for the ways in which I was the wrong mother for her. She gave me a funny look and set the record straight. "You're not the wrong mother for me, Mom," she corrected. "It's just that we balance each other out." (Translation: You're a total mess, but I make it work.)

At least I know that Paige loves me dearly, and even though she gets aggravated with me, I still feel that same bond we've had since she had Michelin baby legs.

And if I fall short as a mother everywhere else, I can always make it up to her in the kitchen: Nothing can turn her into putty like my chocolate chip cookies.

This Christmas, I may give her a big gift card to Hobby Lobby, just to see how much glitter she comes home with.

Mom Report Card

Ways I fell short as a mother	
Bananas. I hate them and forget to buy them.	F
Math. I don't like it and sometimes forgot to teach it.	F
Swimming. I don't own a bathing suit.	F
Animated movies. If the kids watch them, I go do laundry.	F
Late to everything. See previous essay.	F
Daughters' hair. I wasn't into it at all. Sorry, Alex and Paige.	F
Ways I think I got it right	
Laughed a lot.	A
Didn't gossip.	A
Goofed around.	A
Corrected their grammar in text messages.	A
Listened to the Eagles around them.	A
Watched Rodgers and Hammerstein movies with them.	A
Took 'em to church.	A
Loved their dad.	A
Jury's still out	
I was strict about dating. (Maybe it saved them grief? Maybe not.)	???
I worked a lot. (Maybe it taught them to pursue their dreams? Maybe not.)	???
I was kinda messy. (Maybe it taught them to be relaxed? Maybe not.)	???

Misophonia

I have an issue, and until about two years ago I had no idea it was an actual condition with a name. My "little problem," I'll call it, involves being unable to tolerate certain chewing sounds coming from members of my family. It's completely bizarre, and I wish I didn't have it, but by and large it's something I've learned to live with.

The earliest instance of this affliction that I can remember was when I was sixteen, and my then boyfriend, Kevin, in all his Irish Catholic cuteness, took my brother Mike and me out to dinner. The three of us went to China Garden, Kevin's and my favorite restaurant back then, but my much-anticipated order of cashew chicken wound up being completely ruined. Instead of enjoying the flavor of my food, all I could hear was the sound of my brother's chewing, which sounded like the jaws of a vise grinding tighter and tighter. I felt exactly like Emily in *The Exorcism of Emily Rose* when her demon possession was just beginning to show itself and she couldn't bear to sit in the school cafeteria because of the cacophony of utensils clanking and humans eating their food. I remember becoming physically irritated, almost enraged, at Mike's eating—the nerve of him! I didn't want to put anyone on the spot, so I didn't say anything . . . but all I remember from that dinner is a feeling of agitation.

A scene from a random movie was my next sound-related trigger. In *Reversal of Fortune*, actor Fisher Stevens's character was trying to pull one over on Joel Silver's character, and in between sentences, Fisher took a sip of coffee. Only it was the loudest sip/slurp I had ever heard, and even though I loved the movie and watched it over and over because Glenn Close was perfection, I learned that for my sanity, I always needed to leave the room during Fisher Stevens's coffee-drinking scene. That sound! It took me to a dark place that sometimes made me want to punch him. And I had never even met the poor gentleman. He was otherwise a fine actor!

This overwhelming loathing of sound, usually of eating but occasionally not, was unpredictable, and it would hit at the most unexpected moments. From as early as I can remember, loud music in cars always bothered me. I was the party pooper who complained, "Can you please turn that *downnnnnn*?" when my friends blasted the Violent Femmes or Guns N' Roses. I loved the music; I just couldn't handle the volume. They told me I was a lame-o as they loudly munched on Bugles, which of course was another trigger sound and made everything worse. I was such a blast to be around.

As I was raising my children years later, I began to notice that my hatred of certain sounds—and the accompanying overwhelming urge to run out of the house when they began—showed no sign of abating. My sweet Paige would eat a bowl of cereal and my insides would come unglued. My youngest child, Todd, would slurp soup and I could feel my blood start to boil. And don't get me started on Ladd and a can of Pringles. What kind of monster eats a can of Pringles in front of his dutiful, loving wife? I loved him so much every other moment of the year . . . until he ate Pringles. Then I did not want to live with the man at all. Most interestingly, none of my family knew this was happening, because I kept all my consternation inside and seethed quietly. I'm very emotionally healthy in that way.

In a curious twist, I started noticing that this reaction didn't happen during normal, everyday family meals around the table. In fact, those otherwise dreadful, ghastly sounds—the sounds of . . . egads . . . *eating*—didn't bother me at all in the context of dinner. It was only when I was one on one with a kid or Ladd, and they dared to munch or slurp on a snack in my presence, that things in my life fell completely apart.

Still, I chose to be an eardrum martyr and suffer in silence. I surged on in spite of my auditory plight. I figured if I never said anything, I wouldn't introduce the "issue" into my family, it wouldn't become real, and then perhaps I'd stop the cycle, if there even was a cycle. I never remembered my mom or dad becoming enraged when I chewed food as a young child or teenager, and I didn't know where it came from . . . but I still felt a responsibility not to let whatever it was enter into my family's consciousness. Besides, it wasn't every day—it probably happened once or twice a month. But it was still persistent and weird enough that it troubled me.

One day out of the blue, as I was browsing the internet instead of doing laundry, I discovered that the "little problem" with which I was afflicted had a name. The article in front of me described a little-known (at the time, anyway) condition called *misophonia*—which literally translates to (are you ready?) "hatred of sound." It's a disorder in which negative emotions or (sometimes) physical reactions are triggered by certain noises. It's also called "selective sound sensitivity," and I have it, man! I read the signs and symptoms and was immediately certain that this is what I had suffered with and almost (not really, but maybe) punched loved ones over throughout the course of my life. I read celebrity accounts, too! Kelly Ripa, an admitted sufferer, recounted that she almost divorced her husband after listening to him mow down a whole peach one evening. I'd never related to a celebrity so much in my life, and I made a point to mark stone fruits off my grocery list forever. They're so dangerously slurpy, after all.

Since my self-diagnosis day, I've continued my research. The most perplexing thing I've learned about misophonia, and I completely agree with this and can back it up with evidence, is that the most offending sounds tend only to come from those who have the closest relationship with the sufferer. For example, I have never experienced the symptoms (rage and anxiety) of misophonia while having dinner with a casual group of friends. I would never hear a restaurant patron chewing at the table next to me and be overcome with the urge to run screaming from the restaurant. The closer the relationship, the more brutal and amplified the miso-phonic sound—which explains why Ladd eating a can of sour cream and onion chips can cause me to want to take a long walk off a short pier. (I can't exactly explain why Fisher Stevens's coffee slurping set me off, since I hardly knew him. I'll chalk that one up to a misfire.)

The experts aren't exactly sure what causes misophonia. Some believe that a childhood trauma connected to certain sounds might be the trigger. I can't remember such a trauma in my life. Others consider misophonia a sensory disorder. Some experts actually dismiss that it's a real condition! In which case I invite them over to my house and dare them to eat a peach in front of me. Those "experts" won't know what hit them.

Yes, I am a misophoniac—but a highly functioning one. I even came clean to my family about my self-diagnosed condition, so they are aware that it's a thing. But I also work on the cognitive side of things—and if I find myself alone with Ladd while he's devouring chips, and things start to veer off course (i.e., I start plotting his demise or our divorce), I've learned to have discussions with myself. I try to approach things from a logical place: My husband has a right, for example, to sit and eat chips without having to modify the way he eats and somehow figure out how to turn chips into a quiet food. Who needs that pressure? And I make light of it sometimes, too. Recently, when Alex was home on the ranch, she came over and plopped next to me on the sofa with a big cup of ice. After she very loudly munched a couple of mouthfuls, I turned to her and said, "Hey, Alex? Do you really think I'm going to let you sit there and get away with that?"

Alex laughed and kept chomping the ice. I stayed with her and patted her leg because I was so glad she was home, but I was also working out in my head how quickly I could have the ice machine uninstalled from our house. At least we were laughing about it.

In an interesting plot twist, I have come to learn that my sister, Betsy, also suffers from the same condition. She had begun to mention things here and there that involved her son Elliot's eating sounds, and I came clean about the M-word. After doing some research of her own, she thanked me for the diagnosis, because she had been as perplexed about her issue as I'd once been. So now, we are each other's own support group, usually through brief text exchanges, which go something like this:

Betsy: Elliot is eating Grape Nuts. HELP.
Me: Oh no! I'm so sorry! Praying now.

Another recent one:

Me: Paige. Sofa. Macaroni with a spoon.
Betsy: Breathe. Just breathe. Go outside if you
   have to.

And one of the classics:

Betsy: Elliot has a bag of Cheetos and he's licking
   the cheese dust off of each finger one at a time.
Me: Get out of there!!! Save yourself!!!

Our parents must be so proud.

Wannabe Town Kids

Raising kids in the country is great, at least from the perspective of the mother. The growing, developing humanoids have wide-open spaces to play, and they can run around outside in their underwear—or completely naked if they want, but only (by way of Murphy's Law) if the Schwan's man or Orkin man happen to drive up right at that moment. (I deeply apologize to those poor gentlemen through the years. They've seen more than their job descriptions ever called for.)

But anyway, country kids can fish, explore, get dirty, and learn all about nature. In the case of the boys, they can pee outside and not waste water by flushing. (Well, girls can, too . . . it's just . . . oh, never mind.) And if the kids happen to live on a family farm or ranch, they can experience what it means to work the land, contribute to the family business, castrate bull calves, and learn how to be a part of a team working toward a common goal. (I threw in the castrate part to make sure you're paying attention.)

I loved being the mother of country kids. I hadn't grown up in a rural setting and knew nothing about that kind of life until I married my husband, but there was room for them to spread out, and I loved it when they got old enough (say, around two months? Just kidding) to start riding horses and helping Ladd with ranching; I didn't grow up with anything near that level of responsibility, and knew it was going to help shape our kids in innumerable ways. Our four hardly ever complained about ranch work when they were little, which was notable considering they'd sometimes have to get up as early as 3:45 a.m. in the summertime and work elbow deep in grime during long, sweltering days. But every experience—even work—was an adventure for the kids, and they'd always come home with a pocketful of rocks (or calf nuts—see page 255) that they'd collected during their day at the pens. They made incredible memories with their dad, cousins, uncle, and the cowboys in those years . . . and I'd guess they wouldn't change their childhoods for the world.

I use the term "childhood," because once Alex,

my oldest, became a teenager, all of this lovely, rural charm was instantly out the window. Where she'd once bounced out of bed every morning as a cute little cowgirl, eager to get to the barn and saddle her horse, when the teenage years arrived, she became possessed by a demon and getting her out of her bed was suddenly a near-impossible task. Where she once slept in cute PJs with her hands folded neatly and the corners of her mouth turned up in a hint of a smile, she was now a tall, lanky, mushy teenage lump of human Silly Putty, poured into her bed wearing mismatched sweats, with zero desire (or ability) to drag herself out of bed, let alone bounce.

This was an overnight change, as far as her younger siblings were concerned.

"What's wrong with Alex, Mama?" sweet younger sister Paige, all dressed in her working gear, asked. "She won't get out of bed!"

"Is Awex sick?" young Todd asked. "She kinda cwanky."

"No," I answered. "She just needs a little extra boost these days."

"Let's go pour ice water on her!!" Bryce shrieked to his sibs, and they all laughed and ran upstairs in their boots and spurs to do just that. It went over well, as you can imagine. There were punches thrown. Which, of course, made Alex's younger siblings laugh even harder.

But the depth of sleep wasn't the only difference. It was around this time, just over the threshold of adolescence, when Alex had begun to acutely notice the difference between her life on the ranch and that of her friends who lived in town. The switch flipped instantly, around thirteen years old, and suddenly her whole outlook changed. What previously had been a wondrous upbringing on a family ranch was now, instead, her plight. While she was still an upbeat, happy kid most of the time, she could be hit with crashing waves of comparison when she measured the way her summer days were shaping up against those of the "normal" kids in town.

Her friends in town slept in, for example—at least Alex imagined they did. She wanted to sleep in, too. She thought it sounded really, really enjoyable. But again—ranch work became busier than ever during summer, and it wasn't unusual for the kids to have to get up well before daylight four to five days a week for a good two months as Ladd and his brother Tim carried out the work of shipping cattle and weaning calves. Alex was convinced that everyone in town was sleeping until noon every day. "I've never slept until noon in my life," she said. "And it's looking like I never will!" In reality, her friends in town had summer jobs, too, and while they likely weren't getting doused in cold water by their siblings before daylight, it was hardly the Pawhuska sleepfest that Alex was picturing.

As her teenage years continued, Alex also became certain that all the town kids were always attending a 24-7 party that she could never go to because she always had to work cattle the next morning. Even if it was as early as 7:00 a.m. and she was hard at work at the pens, she was certain that all her friends were congregating for a pancake breakfast on a patio somewhere, probably toasting one another with ginger ale in champagne flutes with chilled pomegranate seeds floating on the surface. I gently reminded Alex that her friends couldn't possibly be getting together for a pancake breakfast, because remember—they were all sleeping in until noon? But she couldn't hear me. Teenage angst, fueled by manure and early mornings, can make a girl impervious to logic.

Speaking of that: At a certain point, Alex was completely over manure. She didn't want to see it or be covered in it anymore. Now, this was a concern I could fully understand! No matter how squeaky clean she was when she left the house, she'd come home with a dirty face, muddy boots, and manure-streaked jeans. Her friends in town never encountered manure, she regularly pointed out, let alone found themselves coated with it. "I mean, look at me . . ." She'd demonstrate, pointing at her beyond-sullied person. "Is this even normal?!?" There was always enough irony and barely there humor behind these moments with Alex that I was semi-confident she was in on the joke . . . but the lines are so thin with teenagers, I never knew when she was actually about to snap.

So mostly I just listened. I tried to provide perspective, but what could I say? The kids did, in fact, live on a family ranch, and helping with all the chores and responsibilities is part of the package deal. For a kid on the ranch to sleep in while all the other siblings, cousins, cowboys, and dads are out doing the work would be unheard of. Also unheard of would be doing all of this without getting covered in poop. Poop, like early mornings, is simply part of the package.

In her junior and senior years of high school, Alex got to get out and spread her wings more, playing soccer, hanging with friends, and staying in town at her BFF Meg's if it was too late to drive home to the ranch. Now, she'd still have to drive back home in the morning if there was a big working going on, so she'd always have to weigh the pros and cons of staying out late— but at least she had options. And that's the complicated part of being the mother of a country kid. You want them to have their fun and freedom, but they also have to be there for the work. It's how Ladd had grown up, and I didn't see that he was any the worse for wear. (He's a little baseline in need of a nap all the time, but aren't we all.)

Like clockwork, Paige followed in Alex's footsteps and hit the Silly Putty sleeping stage as well. She grunted a lot, and suddenly had zero use for her siblings, her mother, her boots, her birthright, and manure. And even though I'd just been through the entire process with Alex and had come out the other side, it was no less difficult with Paige—in fact, it was a little more complicated, because Paige was (and is) a natural debater. So instead of simply pointing out the inequities and inadequacies of her adolescence in the boonies and letting it just exist in the ether as a complaint, which was more Alex's style, Paige would actually pose rhetorical questions to me, her mother, who in her mind was somehow responsible for all of these injustices—even though I was quick to point out that it wasn't my fault we lived on a ranch; it was her dad's!

It was the worst at 4:00 a.m.

"Tell me this," she'd grumble, fighting tooth and nail for her right to sleep in. "How can you expect me to get up and work cattle when you never did this as a teenager?" Of course, this only served to infuriate me, especially since I wouldn't have had my coffee yet, and I'd say something like "Yeah, well—I did ballet all the time!! Look at my messed-up toes!" Boy, I sure told her.

And here was an exasperating but brilliant Paige tactic: She'd enroll in online summer classes through a community college so she could say she had school to do on busy workdays. She's a slippery little sucker when she wants to be!

The good news is, the girls made it through, and it didn't take them long after being away from their comfortable nest to appreciate the merits of home. They look back at old photos of the cattle working days with their siblings and cousins, and they laugh and happy-cry at the memories. They jump in and help Ladd on the ranch when they're visiting home, which makes his day every time. And ironically, Bryce and Todd are in the same teenage years now that caused Alex and Paige so much agriculture-related consternation . . . but since they're both seriously pursuing football, they're having to split their focus between that and ranch work, which leaves almost zero time for girls.

And that's just hunky-dory with me!

Special Deliveries

———

We never get UPS or FedEx deliveries at our house on the ranch. This is a harsh reality of country life for me, right up there with no trash service and no meal delivery service and no cable and . . . I'll stop there. Our place is simply too remote, too far off the beaten path, and the drivers for the various carriers have gotten accustomed to leaving our packages in town rather than bringing them all the way out to us. For the longest time, they'd leave our packages on the doorstep of any Drummond residence they happened to encounter in the area; I guess they assumed we all got together for dinner every night and figured our packages would make their way to us pretty quickly. I always used to worry about a distant Drummond cousin opening up my shipment of bras or something.

Around ten years ago, as I was working in my garden, something unexpected happened. I heard the loud rumble of a vehicle and looked down our road to see who was coming. To my shock and surprise, it was a big brown UPS truck—a sight I'd never seen on our property before. I was covered in dirt and tangled in tomato plants, so I simply waved from a distance as the driver hopped out of the truck. "Hi," he said, waving back. "I'm new!" He left a small package on our front porch and, as quickly as he'd appeared, hopped in his big brown truck and drove away. It was the funniest, most random moment, and I just couldn't square it. What in the world? The UPS guy had come to our house! I couldn't wait to tell Ladd. This would totally consume our dinnertime conversation that evening. I might put it in the church newsletter!

Once I'd cleaned the garden mess off my hands, I retrieved the package from the porch and took it in the house. I hadn't been expecting anything specific, but since it was addressed to me, I opened the small box . . . and discovered a teeny, tiny action figurine inside. The thing was smaller than a thimble, the return address was from Japan, and I had no idea what to make of it. So I set the little guy on top of a stack of miscellany on the kitchen counter and went back out to the garden to pull more caterpillars off my tomatoes.

The next day, I got home from a big supermarket run and found—again, to my utter surprise—another UPS package sitting on our front porch. "What in the actual heck," I laughed to myself. "This is insane!" The idea that the UPS truck had made the long drive out to our house the day before was confusing enough; that it had just happened again and that it was only to deliver another single, small package was completely puzzling. I never dared return to the ranch after a trip to civilization without at least eight bags of supplies with me; after living this way for several years, a minuscule delivery like this seemed so inefficient. I opened this second box and found a teeny, tiny helmet that looked suspiciously similar to the action figurine from the day before. When I compared return labels, I saw that it was from the same shipper in Japan. What a (now ongoing) mystery this was!

Over the course of the next ten days, no fewer than eight more small, individual UPS packages would be delivered to my house—yes, on eight different days. When I wasn't home, they were left by the door. When I was home, I insisted to the well-meaning UPS driver that life didn't have to be this way for him. I explained that all drivers before him had made it a practice to leave our packages in town, and in no way did I expect him to regularly make that drive. "That's my job, ma'am," he said with all the conviction of a soldier before driving away from me for the umpteenth time. *He's not going to last to the end of the month,* I thought as I watched the dust trail form behind him.

As for the contents of the eight most recent packages: More figurines. More helmets. A few accessories. All teeny tiny. All meticulously wrapped and shipped individually from Japan. And along the way, I solved the mystery: Seven-year-old Bryce had taught himself how to pull up Amazon on my desktop computer . . . and he and five-year-old Todd had gone on a teeny, tiny action figurine shopping spree (well, the shopping spree wasn't teeny tiny; the figurines were) and had selected the "I want my items as they are available" option—to the detriment of a certain UPS truck's tires. It seems the shipper took that request very literally, and had packed Every. Single. Separate. Piece—bubble wrap, tissue, tape, the works—in different boxes. And the sad thing is, the charges for each of these items were really relatively low. UPS spent way more in airline fuel and gasoline getting them to my house than Bryce—I mean I—ever paid for the items themselves.

I changed my computer password that evening. And the new UPS driver didn't, in fact, last the month. I hope he's happy and well, wherever he is. I haven't seen a brown UPS truck on our homestead since.

Another delivery truck adventure happened a few years earlier, and involved FedEx.

I should back up and explain that all our kids learned how to drive vehicles at a very young age. They drove only on the ranch, never on the highway, and by the time they were six or seven, they were pretty adept at driving around the ranch as needed. One day Alex, our oldest at eight years old, was starting Ladd's big Ford feed truck. He was in the house on a phone call and had asked Alex to take his feed truck to go round up the ranch horses for the next day. As she'd done a hundred times, Alex hopped in the big truck, started it, and waited a couple of minutes for it to warm up.

During that two minutes, in a completely unexpected development, a FedEx truck—which, again, I'd never seen on the ranch before—had not only pulled into our homestead from out of nowhere, it had parked sideways right behind Ladd's big Ford feed truck. At that exact moment, Alex put the truck in reverse and backed up confidently—smashing right into the passenger side of the FedEx truck and leaving an enormous crater. She must have been completely shocked at the collision, considering there had been no one else within twenty miles of the truck when she'd opened the door to get in a couple of minutes earlier. So she did what any normal eight-year-old driver of a big Ford feed truck would do: shifted into drive and quickly fled the scene of the accident. She was so scared and shaken that she didn't know what else to do—so she hid the truck in the cattle pens, then got out and ducked behind the horse barn to hide. On the lam at eight years old. The country can be such a cold, unforgiving place.

Ladd heard the crash and sprinted outside, where he was quite surprised to see a mangled FedEx truck sitting close to where his feed truck used to be, its engine still running. The driver was by now standing outside the truck, physically fine but totally confused.

"Someone just hit my truck and drove off," he said, a dazed look on his face. Just then, out of the corner of his eye, Ladd noticed Alex squat-running back to the house, taking a side route behind the garage. He pretended he didn't see, and helped the driver fill out an accident form. Poor Alex has never gotten over the sound of crunching FedEx aluminum. And again—we've never seen a FedEx truck on our homestead since.

These days, I make it a point to use The Mercantile as our official shipping address. It eliminates confusion, saves fuel, extends the life of tires, and prevents unnecessary insurance claims.

Home delivery isn't always what it's cracked up to be!

Viral Parenting

~

I t was five days after the reality of the Covid-19 pandemic had begun to reveal itself when my entire family returned home to the ranch. Alex's employer in Dallas sent everyone home so they could work remotely, Paige's college classes were moved online, and Bryce's and Todd's school and sports were suspended for the semester. (And we had some extras in the form of my nephew Stuart; Alex's boyfriend, now fiancé, Mauricio; and our foster son . . . more about him later!) So in the matter of less than a week, a comfortable routine I'd just begun to wrap my head around (and become quite fond of)—one that involved my being at home largely by myself all day—was turned on its head.

The first couple of weeks of quarantining with my family were, strangely, kind of wonderful. Despite the scariness we were witnessing on the news, we all were in a bit of a honeymoon period, cooking together using pantry staples, playing board games, and enjoying what really just felt like an extended Christmas break. The kids taught me how to film embarrassing social media videos (which I didn't realize were embarrassing when I filmed them, unfortunately for me), we hung out with the dogs, and we held friendly-but-competitive Texas Hold 'Em poker tournaments a good three nights a week, in which we played for real cash. None of us wore anything fancier than yoga pants—except Ladd, of course, who stayed in his jeans, thank goodness. I'm pretty sure Ladd wearing yoga pants would have signaled the end-times, and we didn't need that stress piled on top of everything else. Along with the rest of the world, we were officially in lockdown mode, and the uncertainty of what the virus was going to mean for everyone's health and well-being only fueled the feeling that it was just us against the world. Family was all that mattered. We would hunker down and get through this together.

The honeymoon started wearing off about three weeks in, when the teenage boys started inquiring about when they could (and why they couldn't) hang with their friends in town. In addition, every couple of days Paige started announcing plans to drive back to her college town to meet up with some of her closest buddies. I'd look at all of them like they were bonkers, which they were. "What are you talking about?!" I'd snap. "We are in a pandemic! There's no hanging! There's no driving! *There are no buddies!*" After a while, I began to resent their asking, as I'd just have to keep giving them the same answer ("absolutely not") every single time, and I couldn't for the life of me understand why they weren't content spending all day playing poker with their middle-aged mother. My kids had all been just fine hanging with me (or I should say *in* me, har har) during their nine months of gestation—surely they could endure quarantine, which hopefully wouldn't last that long?

Other things slowly started creeping in and wearing on my nerves as well. For one, these creatures in my house all wanted to *eat*. As in, food. As in, all the time. I'm not talking about simple ham sandwiches, which are easy, quick, leave very little mess behind, and allow me (a cooking show host, by the way) never to have to cook. No, these hungry life-forms wanted to eat *meals*: proteins cooked in pans, vegetables sautéed in skillets, and potatoes baked in casserole dishes. And, okay, I can understand this to a degree. It's not that unreasonable once a day. But during quarantine, it seemed that as soon as one meal was over and the last dish was in the dishwasher, they'd invariably return to the kitchen for another round. The last straw happened one Sunday, about a month into the lockdown. I'd made blueberry pancakes, fresh fruit salad, scrambled eggs, and bacon for a late morning brunch, and by about 1:00 p.m. the kitchen (which had been completely wrecked by the whole ordeal) was finally clean and the stench that came from frying three pounds of bacon was finally starting to lift. I went to my bedroom to veg and work a crossword puzzle, my quarantine antidote to losing my mind, and then around 2:00 I started hearing banging and sizzling coming from the direction of the kitchen. I investigated and discovered, to my horror, that one of the boys was . . . *frying bacon.*

"What," I barked, "are you *doing*?!?"

Startled, the kid looked up from his skillet and answered, "I'm . . . making a bacon and egg sandwich?" What an absolute animal.

I was utterly and completely dumbfounded. *"Why would you do that?"* I demanded.

"I'm . . . hungry?" he answered. These question marks on the end of statements were starting to tick me off.

"No, you're not," I stated, before ordering him to abort his mission and leave my kitchen (not the family's kitchen, mind you) immediately.

Before I continue, I need to elaborate on bacon in general. It is a beautiful creation and I will love it forever. I am its biggest fan and advocate. But cooking bacon for a houseful of human beings who are all over six feet tall is a no-win proposition. First, you can't cook it fast enough; say you fry eight strips at a time, and each person in your household "sneaks" a piece before the meal is ready . . . and say they do this twice, which is a conservative estimate. In order to accumulate enough bacon to make it to the table, you would have to fry bacon until the year 2028, stopping only for bathroom breaks. Second, cooking that much bacon turns the kitchen into one of those Folgers cans of bacon grease that my grandma Iny had under her stove for forty years. Except all the grease is on the countertop, the stove, the ceiling, and the floor—and not in a can. And third, cooking that much bacon at one time causes the entire house to smell like bacon, and not in a good way. You know when you smell that first spritz of perfume in the mall and you love it, so you buy the large bottle and then wind up hating it because you spray on too much? That's what cooking bacon does to me, minus the floral and citrus notes. So this is why the (nameless, to protect his privacy) teenage boy's bacon and egg sandwich at 2:00 p.m., which followed our sizable Sunday brunch, made me want to blow my stack.

And blow my stack I did. I declared the whole kitchen area a disaster zone and announced that it was closed to the public for the foreseeable future. This madness—this *eating*—absolutely had to stop, I told my family. This careless, reckless snacking and cooking is over, I told them—and they all needed to get on the same eating schedule, and fast. They responded by asking what was for dinner that night.

During the pandemic, I became really good at blowing my stack regularly and making really big declarations. Another involved laundry. My laundry manifesto stated something along the lines of "You all have to do your own laundry from now on because I'm done." A reasonable statement on my part, but it happened so suddenly, no one quite knew what to do. Ladd was a little confused by this sharp turnabout, but he wasn't about to pick this hill to die on. (And he definitely would have died, given my deteriorating state of mind.) A follow-up laundry situation arose about a week later when I discovered that none of the boys had done their laundry but instead had stacked their dirty clothes in their rooms, and I threatened to incinerate (in a beautiful, blazing inferno, I think I said) any dirty clothes I found on the floor from that moment forward. I actually followed through with this a few days later, except I put the dirty clothes in a black trash bag and hid them in my closet, where they still reside today. ("Inciner-ate" means different things to different people.)

God knows I love my family. I'm so grateful that during a time of national crisis, we were able to ride it out and have a period of concentrated togetherness. Being together, after all, did help us process the uncer-tainty and fear. But on the flip side, I see now that I was being slowly driven batty by a complete *lack* of social isolation. I'd notice some of my favorite social media personalities saying things like "I miss hugs" and "I can't wait to be with people." This one in particular stuck out: "I don't ever want to feel this alone again." I would read these posts and absolutely scratch my head. I couldn't relate to them at all. It was all I could do to keep myself from replying publicly with comments like "Yeah, well—I miss solitude, man" and "That's funny that you say that, because I don't ever want to see another person again as long as I live" and "I *long* to feel alone again. How do ya like *them* apples?" This one was a little more obscure, but I considered it, too: "Ban Bacon Forever!!!!!" (I never posted any of this, regrettably.)

Around the sixth or seventh week of being quaran-tined with my family, I actually began to get irritated at the attitude I had developed, and I started looking at the reasons for it . . . or at least a bright side. After much contemplation and a little bit of wine (or maybe I have that backward?) I finally found it: When my girls left for college, I was devastated. I longed for things to be back to the way they were when all the kids were little, back when I was cooking a million meals a day and drowning in laundry and we were all one big, happy, chaotic family. Now, because of a pandemic, I finally had that back . . . and I didn't really want it, at least not on the same scale. And don't get me wrong: I still love being with my children and look forward to many years of Christmas breaks and holiday together-ness. But if there's one thing this time has shown me, it's that motherhood has its many seasons, and I am in the season of loving my children as much as ever, wanting to celebrate their accomplishments and to be a soft place for them to land . . . but needing some dang space.

And needing people to wash their own socks and just eat a ham sandwich from time to time.

THE ABSOLUTE BEST SANDWICH I MADE DURING QUARANTINE

(a.k.a. Drip Beef with Caramelized Onions and Provolone)

Of all the cooking shenanigans that went on in the Drummond kitchen during the 2020 Covid-19 quarantine, this blessed sandwich was the clear winner and received 5+ stars from everyone. It feeds a houseful of hungry teenagers who are depriving you of solitude.

1 chuck roast, about 4 pounds

1 tablespoon kosher salt

1 tablespoon freshly ground black pepper

4 tablespoons (½ stick) salted butter, plus more for the rolls

2 tablespoons vegetable oil

2 cups low-sodium beef broth

2 tablespoons minced fresh rosemary leaves

One 16-ounce jar pepperoncini, including juice

2 large yellow onions, halved and sliced

10 kaiser rolls, split

10 slices provolone cheese

(NOTE: *Can be made in non-pandemic times as well.*)

1. Sprinkle the chuck roast with the salt and pepper. Melt 2 tablespoons of the butter and the vegetable oil in a heavy pot over high heat. Sear both sides of the roast until very browned, about 5 minutes total. Pour in the beef broth and 1 cup water. Add the rosemary, then pour in the pepperoncini with their juices. Cover the pot and reduce the heat to low. Simmer until the meat is tender and falling apart, 4 to 5 hours.

2. Remove the roast from the pot and use two forks to shred the meat completely. Return the meat to the cooking liquid and keep warm.

3. Heat a large skillet over medium-low heat and add the remaining 2 tablespoons butter. Add the onions and sauté until caramelized, stirring occasionally, about 20 minutes.

4. Preheat the broiler. Butter the cut side of the kaiser rolls and toast them in the oven until golden. Set aside the top halves.

5. Spoon some of the shredded meat and juice onto the bottom halves of the rolls. Top each with a slice of provolone, then broil until the cheese is melted and bubbling. Remove the pan from the oven, arrange some caramelized onions on each sandwich, and top with the other halves of the buns.

6. Make your teenagers do the dishes! ☺

The Whole Fam Damily

Sugar Lips

L add's older brother Tim is one of my favorite people—a great guy in every sense of the word. I don't say that in any sort of flippant or insincere way: He truly is a stand-up brother-in-law who would do anything for me or my family, and he and I have never exchanged a single cross word in the nearly quarter century Ladd and I have been married. I think if we ever had any sort of argument or confrontation, we'd probably both start cracking up at the absurdity. That said, Tim has a certain "side" to him that is . . . well, interesting. To paint a little picture of what I'm talking about, I need to go back a bit.

My dad used to tell me a joke he'd heard from some buddies when he was serving as a physician in the Vietnam War. It was a joke about a man named Sugar Lips, who was given his nickname because—the story went—"he had a way with words." If ever there was anyone in town who *always* knew the right thing to say, it was most definitely Sugar Lips—and so when Mr. Brown, a pillar of the community, was tragically hit by a train one day, there was only one person who was equipped to break the news to Mr. Brown's wife. That person, of course, was Sugar Lips. He had a way with words, after all. He accepted the task of delivering the terrible message, and immediately walked to the Brown residence. Sugar Lips gently knocked on the front door, and when a woman opened the door, he asked, "Excuse me . . . are you Widow Brown?"

Confused, the lady at the door replied, "Well, I'm *Mrs.* Brown . . . but I'm certainly not a *widow*."

Sugar Lips looked at her, raised his eyebrows, and replied, "The hell you ain't!!!"

(I could write a whole book about the jokes my dad learned in Vietnam.)

So basically, my brother-in-law Tim is the modern-day Sugar Lips. He definitely has a way with words.

A mere nine and a half months after Ladd and I were married, Tim walked into the hospital room where I was attempting to breastfeed my hours-old baby. Now that the drama and craziness of the middle-of-the-night childbirth process was over and Ladd, the baby, and I had spent a few hours together, I'd sent Ladd home to the ranch a little while earlier to clean up, re-group, and change clothes. Tim knew his brother was heading home for a few hours, so he wanted to come keep me company and meet his new niece Alex, of course. Once I saw that it was him, I hurried to pull up the baby blanket to conceal the reality of the newborn latching-on process, because let's face it—Tim had not grown up with sisters, and knowing my husband's baseline cluelessness about girl things such as this, I didn't want to presume that my brother-in-law had any level of understanding of (or stomach for) female bodily functions.

It was great to see Tim's kind face. He set down a bouquet of carnations he must have snagged in the hospital lobby, then began a casual conversation with me, asking how I was feeling and conveying his excite-ment over becoming an uncle for the first time. He was sweet, but I could also tell he was trying with all his might not to look anywhere south of my face, as it was impossible to ignore the newborn smacks and slurps that were going on under the pastel polka-dotted blanket. It was painfully obvious what was transpiring under there, and he was avoiding it like the plague. He kept looking at the monitor . . . the TV . . . the plas-tic water pitcher on the table near my bed—anywhere but the general vicinity of my bosom. Not that I was eager for my brother-in-law to see anything sensitive, but I felt comfortable that the blanket was an adequate shield. I really wasn't worried about it.

Since it was only day one, there wasn't much milk to be had yet, so I discreetly slipped Baby Alex out from under the boob blanket and presented her to her eager uncle. Bless Tim's heart, he was clearly moved by the moment, and he gave a tender smile before saying "Hey, you" to the new baby in his arms. Then he continued shooting the breeze with me, asking, "So, how long do you plan on breastfeeding her?" I was a little taken aback that he'd just allowed himself to utter such a clinical term.

"Um . . . ," I replied. "I'm really not sure." And I wasn't. I was taking this whole marriage and motherhood adventure one day at a time.

"Well . . . ," he responded. "I just want to let you know, you need to be careful not to get a sour bag." And that was it. He didn't laugh. He didn't smirk. He was serious! And immediately after he said it, he looked down and resumed staring at his newborn niece. Thanks for the livestock lactation advice, Tim.

But this wasn't my first experience with a Tim-ism. Months earlier, just after my previously flat belly had begun to show, Ladd and I had Tim over for dinner.

He greeted us with a smile, but did an obvious double take when he saw me, as it had been a good month since our last visit. I thought maybe Tim was taking notice of my pregnancy glow, or perhaps was thinking to himself how great I looked for someone in the sixth month of pregnancy.

"Oh, wow," Sugar Lips said to me as he entered our kitchen. "For the first time, I can really tell you're pregnant just by looking at your face!" And as he said this, he cupped his hands under his neck, as if cradling some imaginary double (or triple) chin, which he then inexplicably bounced around in his hands. I sort of looked up to the sky at a forty-five-degree angle, pondering the combination of words that had just come out of his mouth. "First time . . . pregnant . . . face." The thing is, Tim was neither kidding, nor being ornery, nor necessarily being inconsiderate. He simply had an honest thought—and when he's around people he knows and trusts, honest thoughts make their way out of his mind and through his lips. His sugar lips, to be exact.

This lack of a filter, I've determined, has to be rooted in cowboy culture, which Tim had been immersed in at an early age. While cowboys are notoriously gentlemanly, when they're in the cattle pens for hours on end they give one another a hard time—usually in the form of brutal honesty. I've observed that most cowboys are able to (pun intended) rein it in when they finish their work for the day and go back into society. But with Tim, that usual cowboy filter just never seemed to develop.

I have countless memories of Tim's Sugar Lips moments through the years, and to know him is to understand and love him. But what is perhaps my favorite Sugar Lips story occurred very early on, at Ladd's and my wedding. Sally, the daughter of an area rancher who at one time had been engaged to Tim (they'd mutually called it off a few months before their wedding date), was in attendance, and by now she had not only married a different cattleman, she was eight months pregnant with their first child. Tim hadn't heard the pregnancy news, but when he saw Sally at the reception, he greeted her with a hug and asked her all about how she and Kent, her husband, had been doing. The exchange was a little awkward considering their relationship had ended in a broken engagement a handful of years before, but he went out of his way to make her feel comfortable, which Tim is (very ironically) really good at doing.

"Man, Sally," he said after a few minutes. "Looks like you've put on a little weight!" He chuckled a little, as he and Sally had always had a jokey relationship that involved jabs and teasing. At this point, Tim still didn't know she was expecting. (I told you . . . he didn't have sisters.)

But Sally wasn't chuckling back. Her eyes turned into lethal lasers, the kind that could only emanate from an angry gestating female, and she fixed them on Tim, her prey, before replying with four beautiful, crystal clear words: "I'm *pregnant*, you *idiot*!!" Then she stalked off, found her husband, and enjoyed the rest of her evening.

Today, despite the wrinkle with Tim, Sally and her husband are close friends with our whole family. Tim is happily married to Missy, and they have two grown children. Missy does a stellar job keeping Sugar Lips in check by both celebrating his naïvely indelicate nature and kicking his shin under the table when the need arises. And what Tim burns to the ground with his very occasional faux pas, he more than makes up for with random acts of kindness.

Oh, and an update! I never did get that sour bag Sugar Lips warned me about. It sure is a good thing he said something.

Drummond Family Nicknames

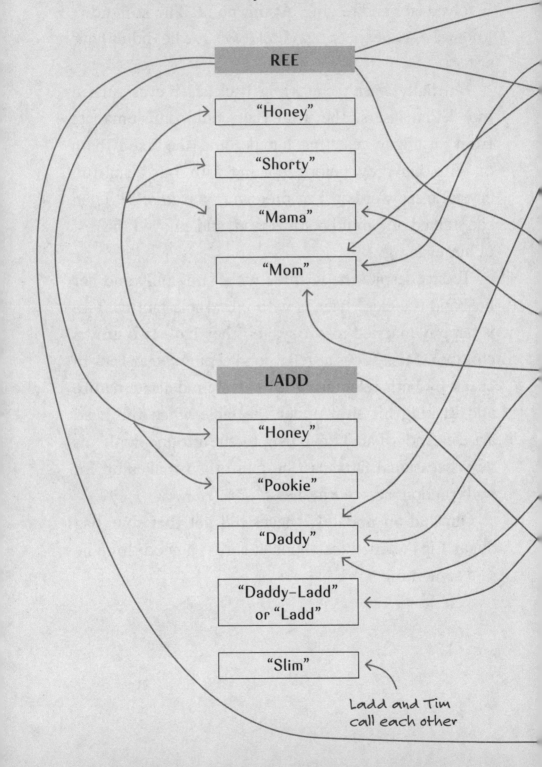

REE

"Honey"

"Shorty"

"Mama"

"Mom"

LADD

"Honey"

"Pookie"

"Daddy"

"Daddy–Ladd" or "Ladd"

"Slim"

Ladd and Tim call each other

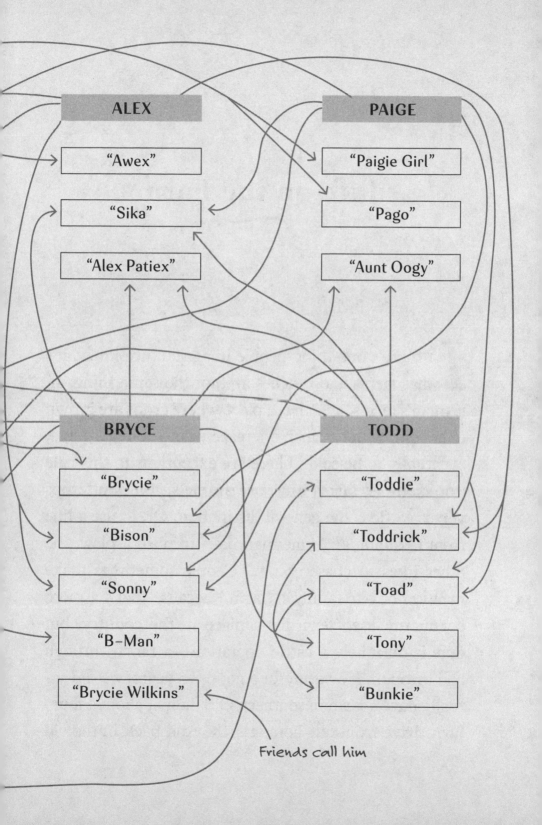

ALEX

"Awex"

"Sika"

"Alex Patiex"

PAIGE

"Paigie Girl"

"Pago"

"Aunt Oogy"

BRYCE

"Brycie"

"Bison"

"Sonny"

"B–Man"

"Brycie Wilkins"

TODD

"Toddie"

"Toddrick"

"Toad"

"Tony"

"Bunkie"

Friends call him

Life on the Farm

~

*I*f there's one thing people in agriculture know, it's that farms and ranches are not the same thing. In layman's terms, a farm is a place where crops are grown to be sold, while a ranch is a place where animals graze, eventually to be sold. There are exceptions to this rule (for example, farms can raise animals, too), but crops versus cattle is the general distinction. Or, to use a line from *Oklahoma!*: "One man likes to push a plow, the other likes to chase a cow." People sometimes make mention of our family's "farm" because that's a more commonly used term for a place in the country, but ours is definitely a cattle operation—a ranch through and through. However, for a good ten years, we *did* actually have a farm in southern Oklahoma, about a four-hour drive from our home ranch. And back in the old days, for about three weeks every summer, the whole fam damily—Ladd, me, Tim, Missy, my in-laws, and all the kids—would head there together for some concentrated, cramped, crazy *Green Acres*-style fun.

The farm in southern Oklahoma grew only wheat, but not for the purposes of harvesting and selling. It was planted solely to graze cattle on—an alternate approach to the way we do things here on the ranch, where cattle graze on the grass that grows naturally. There's no huge difference in the end result of cattle that graze on wheatgrass versus regular grass; it just diversified our resources a bit—in other words, you should really ask Ladd to explain, because I have no idea what I'm talking about. (I tried.) Effectively, our farm in southern Oklahoma was pretty much a ranch with some wheat pasture—but we called it the farm to keep things simpler. Anyway, while Ladd, Tim, and their dad, Chuck, took regular short trips to the farm throughout the year, a three-week continuous stretch in the summertime was always necessary so they could knock out a bunch of intensive work in a short period of time.

During those summer stretches, the mom (Nan), the wives (Missy and me), and the six kids would pack up and head south with them. The menfolk needed the company of their ladies down there, after all. Oh, and the menfolk needed food—lots and lots of food. Finally, the menfolk most certainly needed extra hands in the form of their offspring; it's a well-known fact that people in agriculture (whether farmers or ranchers) procreate not just to carry on the family name, but to ensure a stronger, more dedicated workforce. Ladd neglected to tell me this when he proposed.

We've since sold our farm, and because of this, the memories from that place are so precious to me. The kids were all very young when we took these farm trips, and in the late afternoon, after all of the work was done, we'd sit out on the porch and watch the kids run around and play. The workdays were long, hot, and grueling, so Nan fashioned a makeshift swimming pool out of a big fiberglass horse trough so the kids could splash around and cool off—sometimes in their underwear, often less. Missy would drink sweet tea, I'd sip white wine, and Nan would smoke cigarettes, and we'd just sit and soak up that relaxing feeling that comes when you're far away from all the chores of home. Never mind that we had just as many chores down at the farm; somehow they felt like vacation chores to us.

What didn't feel like vacation was how early we had to get up during these farm trips. Since it was the height of summer—and in hot, dry southern Oklahoma, no less—the guys had to start work especially early so they could avoid working cattle in the hottest part of the day. That level of heat is hard on the working crew, but it's even harder on the animals. So on a typical morning on the farm, the alarms would start blaring at about 3:30 a.m., and then the hellish grind would begin: We'd wake up the kids, get them all to brush their teeth, round up their work gloves, socks, jeans, shirts, boots, and hats. Half the clothes would still be in the dryer from the night before, and we'd always curse ourselves for not laying it all out before bed, but of course we'd all been too exhausted. Some would wake up chipper, others would wake up cranky and cross—and that's just the adults I'm talking about. The kids would display the same range of moods, and by the time they all headed out on their horses about forty-five minutes later, I felt like I'd been put through the wringer.

I should point out that at our house on the farm, the layout was such that Tim's family of four shared one bedroom, our family of six shared another bedroom . . . and the two were connected by a single Jack-and-Jill bathroom, God have mercy upon us. (Chuck and Nan had their own bedroom and bathroom, but they'd kinda earned that luxury.) Today, considering that three of my four children are more than six feet tall, I can't conceive of such a sardine-esque arrangement . . . but even back then, ten humans sharing one bathroom was an exercise in patience and insanity, and I truly can't believe we're all still speaking to one another. I mean, who would have thought that when I happened to wake up at 1:00 a.m. to go to the bathroom that one night, my brother-in-law would have already had the same notion? (Learn to lock the door, Tim!) And I can recall two separate times that Missy walked in while Ladd was showering. Why do bad things happen to good people? Again, I can't believe we're all still speaking.

Sometimes, to get away from the house for a bit in the late afternoon, I'd leave the kids with Nan and ride along on the ATV with Ladd when he went to check on the cattle. The scenery was unbelievably gorgeous—vast fields of fresh wheatgrass in the most saturated kelly green you've ever seen, with Black Angus cattle scattered here and there like polka dots. On the flip side, the smells were really, really gross. I'd begun to notice that cow manure at the farm smelled much stronger—and much, much worse—than cow manure on the ranch. Not that cow manure ever smells like roses, but something was amiss here. It was concentrated and overwhelming, like an entire can of cow-manure-scented air freshener had been emptied in one go. After my ninetieth comment on the stench, Ladd finally told me that it was because of the wheat, which has a certain composition of nutrients that makes manure particularly malodorous. Only he explained this fact using three simple words, as only Ladd can do: "Wheat shit stinks." My husband has always had a way of cutting to the heart of the matter.

We had birthday parties at the farm. For reasons I don't want to analyze too much, several of the Drummond kids have summer birthdays, so we'd bake chocolate sheet cakes, get balloons at the local gift shop, and wrap gifts ranging from life-size Hulk hands to shiny new monogrammed spurs. Tim would always chase down the birthday kids and give them swats, one for every year of their life—doubling that number if they screamed or resisted. One summer, we'd been too busy to make a sheet cake for Todd's birthday, so we went to the local supermarket and grabbed premade cupcakes with icing so blue it actually glowed. I still swear that the blue food dye must have been faulty, or a novice baker must have added too much, because all twelve of us had bright blue lips and tongues for the rest of our time at the farm. The cowboys were worried we'd experienced a radioactive event at the house when they showed up to work the next morning—but we explained that Todd's Cookie Monster birthday cupcakes were to blame.

Everything was more concentrated at the ranch: living quarters, manure smells, blue food coloring . . . and weather. Storms at the farm always seemed much more volatile and violent than the ones at the ranch, and one evening toward the end of a summer stay, a wicked one started brewing. It came from out of nowhere, and once Ladd, Tim, and Chuck saw the amount of rain that was falling, they looked concerned. Turns out some cattle they'd worked that day were grazing in a tricky spot on the farm that's prone to flooding, so they hurried to saddle their horses and head to the remote spot.

Minutes after they pulled away with their horse trailer, the sky above the house turned a disturbing shade. Anyone from the Midwest knows this color well—it's a mix of pink and gray, with a little green and dread mixed in. It only happens when the oxygen is being sucked out of the atmosphere by a forming tornado, and it always strikes fear in the heart. Nan, Missy, and I tried to check the radar, but the satellite was down and smartphones hadn't quite been born yet. So as the wind picked up, we gathered the kids and took them to the pantry, the most interior room of the house, to hunker down. Chuck called right after we pulled the door closed, and told us that Ladd and Tim's horses were belly deep in water as the brothers were trying, in lightning and stinging rain, to herd the cattle to safety. Chuck wanted us to check the weather—which we couldn't do. Then the call dropped and we had no choice but to wait. And pray. (And eat the whole box of graham crackers on the bottom shelf.)

Thankfully, everything turned out okay that evening. The brothers got all the cows to higher ground, and got themselves and their horses safely out of the storm. There was a confirmed tornado at the farm, but it only briefly touched down in an open pasture that was nowhere near the house. The men and the women had braved the storm in two very different ways, and all the creatures under both of our care were safe. And later, when everyone was back home under the same roof, we spent a few minutes swapping stories of our respective experiences . . . but that was only the beginning of that night's adventures.

We still had to fight over who got to take the first shower . . .

Did She Just Say "Dick"?!?

One of the most defining characteristics of my mother-in-law, Nan, was her mysterious combination of sophisticated elegance and rural, no-nonsense practicality. Physically speaking, she was a supermodel-level stunner: almost six feet tall, thin and willowy, with an innate sense of style that could only be described as God-given. She'd throw on a knee-length camel coat with slim jeans, a fitted tee, a perfect scarf or beads (or both) that tied it all together, and then slip some kind of tasteful animal-print mules on her size 10 feet. If I'd tried to wear what she was able to pull off, it would have been just sad, but Nan completely rocked everything she wore. She carried herself with the kind of grace that suggested a well-behaved, cultured upbringing. Her soft-spoken nature only added to the allure.

All of this fashion sense and refinement belied the fact that Nan had grown up on a large cattle ranch in a vast, isolated area of northern Oklahoma. Save for her parents, two siblings, and one beloved Border collie, she didn't have a lot of daily interaction with other humans. A lover of the outdoors, she generally helped her dad with the ranching operations, tilled and weeded his enormous garden, and spent her spare time staring at the clouds and thinking about her future traveling the world. (Spoiler: She married my father-in-law in college and moved straight to his ranch thirty miles from where she grew up. Life is weird.)

I started to notice this juxtaposition with Nan—this mix of otherworldly elegance and country girl pragmatism—as the first year of my marriage to her son unfolded, but my younger sister, Betsy, while visiting me one weekend, was treated to a delicious crash course. Betsy's experience with my mother-in-law had been, up until that point, centered around wedding events and the kinds of get-togethers that two families engage in when they're becoming acquainted. Her perception of Nan was skewed heavily toward the elegant side of the continuum; she saw her as a beautiful woman, polished and pure, which of course she was. Until she wasn't.

It was the dead of winter when Betsy came for her

visit, and Nan had invited us to drop by her house on the ranch to have some hot chocolate and say hi. After hugs and niceties, the three of us sat down at the kitchen island, where Nan served cocoa in her grandmother's china. Considering it was a bitter-cold day, she began to regale us with memories and stories that took place on the ranch in previous winters, and Betsy and I settled in for what we thought would be a collection of idyllic tales involving snowmen, toasting marshmallows, and horses wearing hand-knit argyle sweaters.

Nan's first story (which wound up being the only story) involved one winter many years earlier, when the temperature dropped quickly and wound up setting record lows. A wintry mix of heavy snow and slick ice covered the countryside, and while horses and cattle are surprisingly tough in such conditions, care has to be taken to make sure the animals have all they need to weather the storm. My father-in-law worked the ranch himself, with no cowboys except his three very young sons, and to ensure his livestock withstood the cold snap, he had to take hay and feed to all the pastures so the animals would have nourishment and warmth to get them through a brutal, blizzardy forty-eight hours. "I went out to help him," Nan explained, "and when we got to the South Big South [a pasture on the ranch], we saw a bull standing perfectly still and not following along with the others." Evidently the bull looked like he wanted to join his bovine friends, but for some reason, he wasn't able to take any steps. "How sad," Betsy and I both remarked. "Was he sick? Confused? Crippled?" (Another spoiler: He was none of those things.)

"Chuck and I finally pulled up to him in the feed truck and got out," Nan continued, her lithe fingers tucking her pewter hair behind her ear. "And it turned out that the bull's dick was frozen to the ground."

Come again?

"Wait . . . what?" I asked, setting down my teacup.

"The bull's dick was frozen to the ground," she repeated.

Betsy's hands gripped her cocoa more tightly. "Wait . . . what?" she asked. I was glad she chimed in, too, because I didn't want to ask a second time.

"The bull's dick was frozen," Nan said again. "It was frozen to the ground." It was like she was speaking to two young women who didn't understand the language or dialect she was using, and she thought that by simply repeating it, they would somehow be able to assimilate the horror of what they had just heard. And the thing is, Nan wasn't laughing. She wasn't trying to be funny. She wasn't trying to shock us. She was matter-of-factly informing us that a bull in the South Big South, through some turn of events I'm still not sure I understand, had been caught unprepared when the temperature dropped suddenly, and a certain part of his anatomy had come in contact with the icy ground. And the two (the bull and the ice) were joined together in a very unholy matrimony.

But Nan wasn't finished. "We tried to chip away the ice, but his dick wouldn't budge. We were afraid his dick would get frostbite, so we wound up getting thermoses of warm water from the house and pouring it on the ice until his dick came loose." *Dick, dick, dick.* I'd never before heard the word "dick" so many times in short succession in my life. Betsy's eyes were the size of the saucers underneath our teacups of now-tepid cocoa, since the bull story had gone on for quite a while. There were explanations of why the bull's . . . anatomy had been so close to the ground to begin with, and what happens to a cow's teats when the same fate strikes, and I was queasy by the time it was all over. Ultimately, Nan's story had a happy ending: All the livestock on Drummond Ranch got through that snowstorm okay, including the bull and the various aspects of his . . . anatomy.

It wasn't that my sister and I had never heard the word before. It wasn't that the word offended us. It was that Nan used it with such conviction, and in such a clinical, matter-of-fact way. And that she looked like a supermodel while using it. It was all so fascinating. I, for one, didn't see that story coming. When our visit concluded, Betsy and I gathered our things. Nan gave her a big hug and told her she hoped she'd come visit more often.

Once we were in my vehicle and I started the ignition, my little sister had but one comment: "Did she just say 'dick'?"

Hop Aboard the
Chuck Wagon

My father-in-law's name is Chuck. He's one of a kind, a rare breed, and he definitely makes life more interesting. (And exciting! And unpredictable.) I consider myself to have completely lucked out in the father-in-law department, and I wouldn't trade him for the world. Still, being a part of Chuck Drummond's life is a little bit of a ride. I'm not exactly sure what kind of ride it is, either. A roller coaster would be too volatile. A merry-go-round would be too calm. So I'll just say it's a never-ending trail ride . . . but on this trail ride, the Chuck Wagon is leading the way.

Anyone who's seen Chuck on my TV show (and certainly anyone who's met him in person) knows he has a distinctive voice that's impossible to mistake for any other. It's rough, coarse, raspy, and gravelly. Reports from the old days indicate that no babies could stay asleep on Drummond Ranch as long as Chuck was on the premises. It's hard to describe it in words and really has to be experienced to be believed, but imagine placing a normal male voice in a blender, then adding rocks, tobacco, scrap metal, diesel fuel, and a shot of whiskey, then pulsing for a few seconds. And that is the sound that comes out of my sweet father-in-law's mouth when he speaks, whether he's expressing love, spinning an old yarn, or barking an order to someone on the ranch. His voice does come in handy, because we always know when he's in the room. (Or, let's face it, county.)

My father-in-law cherishes his family, particularly his grandchildren. He requested twelve and got six, so he has twice the amount of love for each of them. Now, this doesn't mean that he's treated his grandkids with kid gloves . . . on the contrary, he started taking them to work with him on the ranch when they were very young, and he expected them to work even harder than the cowboys. He taught them the ropes, and he wasn't afraid to give them on-the-job "training" (using the voice I described above) if they weren't moving fast or trying hard enough. I'm convinced this toughened the spirits (and sharpened the skills) of all the Drummond grandchildren, girl and boy alike, in a way that nothing else could. If you can withstand a hollering grandpa whose voice sounded like it was birthed in a rock quarry, you can face most anything in life.

Speaking of taking the kids with him, it's always been Chuck's firm belief that guys on a ranch should never, ever have long hair. This is purely practical from his perspective: Long hair gets too hot, it looks messy, it collects dirt and grime, and it doesn't serve a purpose, which is basically Chuck's measure for everything. He himself has had a buzz cut since 1957, back when they were actually in style, so to him, it's really the only haircut a man (or boy) needs to have. As my two boys were growing up, I learned the hard way never to get too attached to their soft wavy curls, because if they spent more than two hours with Chuck, he'd run them by the barber shop to get a fresh buzz. Even today, now that both Bryce and Todd are fully in charge of their own hair destiny, their grandpa still threatens to haul them down to the barber shop (or cut it in their sleep) if they let it get too long. They know he means it, too.

Chuck is nothing if not a miracle; my son Todd says, "Pa-Pa's invincible and is gonna live forever, as long as he has all the Baby Ruths and Diet Pepsi he needs." He smokes two packs a day and has had two bypass surgeries, a shoulder replacement, a broken neck, two kinds of cancer, eye surgeries, and several other ortho-

pedic procedures. He takes a licking but keeps on ticking, just like an old Timex watch. And he doesn't really
believe in sleeping much: "The human body really
only needs ninety minutes of sleep per night," he once
told me. He believes this, by the way (even though he
definitely gets a little more than that in reality), and
no amount of newfangled data about the importance
of REM sleep and the health benefits of a good eight
hours a night will sway his real-life experience. He
eats too much sugar, gravy is his favorite food group,
and Diet Pepsi is his coffee every morning. He really
shouldn't have lived as long as he has . . . but I'm so
very, very grateful he has.

Chuck and I share a love of food, but his love bor-
ders more on obsession. I've never seen a person so
motivated by what he's going to eat each day; while
he's finishing up one meal, he starts thinking (and asking) about what his next meal's going to be. He is literally incapable of keeping himself from eating a slice of
pecan pie the night before Thanksgiving, and by a slice,
I mean he's eaten half of a Thanksgiving pie the night
before, then panicked about what he was going to tell
Nan the next morning. My mother-in-law used to quietly phone and ask me to limit the chocolate sheet cakes
I made for Chuck, because he always had a hard time
not eating half of it in one sitting and she couldn't bear

to watch it. He and Nan were completely mismatched in this regard, as she hardly cared about food at all. And somehow, in a cruel twist of fate, she married a man who liked to have hours-long conversations about it. Bless her. I like to think she's enjoying Heaven, not just for the obvious reasons (paradise and all), but also because she doesn't have to talk about food with Chuck anymore.

My father-in-law's generosity has always been one of his trademarks. When Ladd and I were engaged, Chuck began gifting me with iron skillets. They weren't wrapped in gift packaging or given to me at any sort of wedding shower or occasion. He'd just hand them to me in passing, saying something along the lines of "Here, I got you an iron skillet." He was simply building the arsenal that he knew I would eventually need on the ranch in order to survive. Over the years, I began to notice that the skillets were getting bigger. The last one he gave me won't even work on a normal home stove; the only way a person could have a fighting chance of cooking with it is over a large inferno at a campout. Chuck knows I'm not big on camping, but he isn't even trying to get me to camp. He was just uncomfortable knowing that there was a size or shape of iron skillet in existence that I didn't yet own. Ditto on all the over-size spatulas, slotted spoons, and potato mashers he's thrown my way. Practical gestures are Chuck's primary love language.

Along those lines, my father-in-law has always been supportive of my career endeavors. When my first cookbook was released many years ago, I was invited to appear on QVC (the home shopping channel) to promote it. This was one of my very first TV appearances, and Chuck made sure he was home and parked in front of his TV thirty minutes in advance of my segment. The show I appeared on was *In the Kitchen with David,* a popular Sunday special that features pots, pans, appliances, and clever kitchen gadgets galore . . . and not only did he watch my six-minute segment, he also watched all the other segments on David's three-hour show. By the time the episode was over, Chuck had called QVC and placed orders for three of every single pot, pan, appliance, and clever gadget he had seen that day—a set for me, a set for him, and a set for my sister-in-law, Missy. The boxes arrived daily over the following two weeks, and I still have that darn pineapple slicer today. It sure is handy when I can remember to use it.

Excess generosity is never more at play with Chuck than in the summertime, when farm stands start popping up in Oklahoma and Kansas. He loves driving out into the great beyond and coming back with a produce haul, whether it's fresh corn, ripe tomatoes, or juicy peaches. Of course, he lives alone now and though he does enjoy cooking for himself, he only needs a small handful of each—but Chuck would never be content buying three or four ears of corn at a time. So I'm usually the lucky recipient.

"Ree," he grumbles over the phone. "I'm heading out to get some corn . . . you want some?"

"Oh . . . well, yes, Chuck! I'd love that!" I respond. I do this not because I love fresh corn (I do), but because there's no way I could bear to crush his spirit by saying no. But then I regret not saying no, because a few hours later he'll park his pickup by my back door and tell me he got me twenty dozen ears or something. I thank him and cook or freeze what I can, but often wind up divvying out what I can't use to friends and organizations. I guess the whole purpose of the exercise is for Chuck to have a reason to go buy truckloads of produce, because giving a loved one fresh produce really is one of his true joys in life. I guess that's worth my making a few extra stops to drop off corn around town.

My father-in-law is a rolling stone, resolved not to collect a hint of moss. Chuck is happiest being busy and having tasks, certainly since Nan passed away, but the truth is, he's always been like this. Ladd and his brother Tim joke—but they aren't really joking—that they try really hard to make sure Chuck has plenty of regular ranch work, fence work, and improvements to supervise, because if he doesn't, he'll create an enormous project just to have the work to do—and he'll hire five or six guys to help him get it done. "Dad creates work," they say, shaking their heads. They've lived it their whole lives.

Or, even better, he'll locate a little piece of land that he thinks Ladd or Tim should buy, and he'll "accidentally" make an offer on their behalf without talking to them first. It's often said about Border collies that if they don't have a job or activity, they can get destructive. Well, if Chuck doesn't have a job or activity, things can get expensive. I try always to help out by telling Chuck if I have any needs, large or small, around our homestead. I'd rather he bring me a little dirt for a raised flower bed than decide to rebuild all the fences on Drummond Ranch. (He probably has sketches of those fence plans in his bedside table.)

Ladd and Tim are grateful to have learned so many invaluable lessons from their dad. He's a true old-time rancher, and as much as he likes to keep things stirred up around here, there's no one who knows more about the cattle business than Chuck. The Drummond kids all think Pa-Pa is a legend—and I agree. My eyes always light up and my heart leaps a bit when I see him—because he's such a huge life-force in our family.

He's been through it all, he's seen it all, and while we sometimes have to laugh at the larger-than-life character that is our dad/grandpa/father-in-law, we make it a point to cherish the moments . . . the conversations . . . the stories.

And the corn. Always the corn.

A Tale of Two Families

I grew up on a golf course.
Ladd grew up on a cattle ranch.

My dad doesn't own a pair of jeans.
Ladd's dad irons creases in his jeans.

I spent summers swimming at the pool.
Ladd spent summers working on the ranch.

My dad put artificial hips in patients.
Ladd's dad pulled calves out of cows.

I slept till noon on Saturday.
Ladd slept till 6:00 a.m. on Saturday.

The Smiths had a service pick up their trash.
The Drummonds burned their trash.

My mom cooked for the church youth group.
Ladd's mom cooked for hungry cowboys.

My mom took us to church.
Ladd's mom took them to church.

I went to operas with my mom.
Ladd went camping with his mom.

My mom borrowed eggs from the neighbors.
The Drummonds didn't have any neighbors.

The Smiths ate dinner at six o'clock every night.
The Drummonds ate dinner whenever they got
    home from working on the ranch.

The Smith kids got their driver's licenses at sixteen.
The Drummond kids started driving at six.

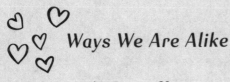

Ways We Are Alike

* Lots of love
* Moms were tall
* Movie fans
* Football fans
* Moms were great cooks
* Dads worked a lot
* Both families went to New York City to see
  Broadway shows in the summer of '82.
  (Smith kids loved it; Drummond kids didn't.
  Ha ha.)

A Rich Inner Life

It's been two years since we lost Nan, my mother-in-law, to cancer. It was terrible and awful, and it's taken our family a while to dig out of the grief . . . but I've found that over time, the hole in my own heart can easily be filled by accessing a special little bank of Nan memories that I'd been saving away since she entered my life over twenty-five years ago. Man, was she a dandy.

I was lucky to have been the first real daughter figure in my mother-in-law's life. She'd raised three sons in the country, and while there was a bit of a learning curve before she knew exactly what to do with me, we very quickly became good friends. Back in the early years of my marriage, Nan would call me (on a landline, mind you) almost every morning. I remember a few months after our wedding, I told Ladd that I'd figured out that if I wasn't necessarily in the mood to chitchat early in the day (and I sometimes wasn't), I'd better not pick up the phone, because I'd be in for a good hour-long conversation with his mom. Her calls usually came before 8:00 a.m.

But the thing of it was, what Nan wanted to talk about usually wasn't trivial. I always think about the Eleanor Roosevelt quote, "Small minds talk about people; average minds talk about events; great minds talk about ideas." On my mother-in-law's morning calls to me, she definitely talked about ideas. Maybe it was as simple as the color wheel and what made her tick in terms of primary and secondary hue combinations— and how her love of nature drove which colors she chose to wear or decorate her house with. Maybe it was about a scripture, or a story from her rural childhood, or an observation she'd made about the way animals interact with each other at different times of year. I never knew what topic was waiting for me on the other end of the line. It was a surprise smorgasbord every time.

Nan told me stories about when she first met Chuck, the son of a rancher in a neighboring county—how he gave her and her cousins a ride home from college one weekend, how he kept checking her out in the rearview mirror during the eighty-mile drive, how she decided that he (at five foot eight) was way too short for her (five eleven), and besides that, he was sure to go into his family's ranching business . . . and that was *definitely* not what she wanted to do with her life. Nan wanted to travel the world, join the Peace Corps. She had things to do, places to see.

She told me how Chuck eventually won her over with his perseverance. When they were dating and he would drive to visit her on her own family's ranch, he'd have to pack three spare tires because he'd almost always get at least one flat on the way. Nothing was going to stop him from seeing her, and she was attracted to that determination. She talked a lot about their marriage: What it was like being married to a "determined" workaholic rancher, and how important she felt it was for her to be Chuck's strongest support. She said to me that she watched how hard Chuck worked, how much he struggled to keep the ranch together during some very difficult years, and how discouraged he would sometimes get. "I always felt like it was my job to dust him off, prop him up, and give him strength so he could go right back out into battle the next day," she'd tell me. Being a wife (and fierce ally) to Chuck was Nan's life's work—this was so clear. It was her holy calling. As a young wife, this set a powerful example for me.

My mother-in-law had a rich inner life, which gave

birth to some far-flung theories. For example, she launched a yearslong effort to paint everything on the Drummond homestead in browns and other earth tones so that (her words) if enemy aircraft ever flew overhead (in rural landlocked Oklahoma, mind you), the house and barns wouldn't easily be spotted. This was the opposite of everything Chuck and his sons believed in: Fences and pens were always to be painted bright white, and they loved to slap bright red metal roofs on barns and other outbuildings. But not Nan, who was so intent on blending in—not just in a crowded room, but at her exact longitude and latitude. "You just never know!" she always said. Ladd and I live on their old homestead now, and I still peek out the window with unease if I hear the sound of a plane. It makes me laugh, and it makes me miss my mother-in-law.

Nan, a devout Christian who read the Bible but steered clear of religious institutions in her later years, was suspicious of movies that featured any goblin or ghoul that won the heart of a child. So whether it was E.T. or Casper the Friendly Ghost, my mother-in-law was skeptical. She posited that if there was a Satan, and she believed there probably was, he could possibly reach people by desensitizing them to demons and evil spirits during their childhood. She wasn't saying this was proven or even necessarily that she believed it . . . but Nan was happiest living in a world of possibilities, where she was basically optimistic but always curious, sometimes dubious and suspicious. I listened to these theories of hers with great interest. I thought some bordered on wacky, but I loved the way her mind worked. She looked at things in such a nonlinear way.

She had her unintentional funny side: Nan inexplicably referred to electric back massagers as "vibrators" and didn't seem to understand that the word she was using was usually reserved for a very different kind of electronic device. When she and I were helping to clean out the house of her own mother-in-law, Ruth, after she moved to a retirement community, we discovered an entire hallway cabinet filled with nothing but back massagers. These are often given as one-off Christmas gifts, and Ruth's entire family network must have been under the impression that she suffered from chronic muscle tension, because there were thirty of them, minimum, in all shapes and sizes. Because Nan was responsible for divvying up decades of Ruth's belongings to family, I listened over and over as she called Ruth's grandchildren individually and asked them to come by and grab three or four of their grandmother's vibrators. I loved my mother-in-law so much, and I respected her, and correcting her was never something I wanted to do. So I just let her do (and say) her thing.

(The mystery and brilliance of Nan was that I was never 100 percent sure she wasn't in on the joke. But no mere mortal would ever be able to tell.)

One time when Nan, my sister-in-law Missy, and I were flying to Denver for a cookbook signing, I passed Nan a (quarter-size) Airborne tablet along with a bottle of water. "Break it in half," I told her, intending for her to dissolve it in the water so that it could be drunk. A minute later I saw Nan across the aisle of the airplane, head near her knees with her hand over her mouth. Afraid she was having some kind of attack, I leapt over to her and saw that foam was pouring from her lips. She'd broken the tablet in half and swallowed it—with a big swig of Sprite instead of water. I guess she'd never heard of Airborne before that day. She burped the whole trip.

Nan said "humble" with a silent "h" but she pronounced the "h" in "herbs." And she sounded out every word and syllable of "Worcestershire" (wore-sess-ter-shi-yer) because she assumed the correct pronunciation (worse-ter-shur) was people just being lazy with their speech. She never wore the same solid color of pants and shirt (whether black, red, or white) because she was very tall and very thin, and said she never wanted to look like a column. I could go on and on and on.

Nan's life was defined by family, and was forever changed when she lost her oldest son. Todd, Ladd's brother, was killed in a car accident a couple of months before he was set to head to college (Ladd was a young teen when it happened). I never knew Todd, so Nan filled in the blanks about him—who he was and the loss she suffered when he died. Sometimes she'd mention it in a passing, wistful thought; other times, she'd let the tears flow. She told me that when Todd died, she responded in the months and years that followed by rejecting anything in life that she perceived as trivial: She dug up all her flower beds and removed decorative color and patterns from her house. She stopped playing bridge and gave up going to social events in town because she just didn't see the point of idle chatter when her whole world had been upended.

I married Ladd about twelve years after Todd's death, and over the following years, as grandchildren came and her family grew, I got to witness the beauty of real joy slowly entering a grieving woman's life again. Sure, the pain was always close to the surface and could be triggered by a song or a memory. But she'd also laugh, tell jokes, go to dinner, take the grandkids shopping—and I would occasionally watch her and marvel. *She has lost a child,* I'd think, *and look at her over there enjoying life.* I was always grateful to her for demonstrating to me what that kind of strength really looks like.

From all our phone calls and car rides and other one-on-one conversations, I knew that Nan was very interested in the subject of Heaven. After Todd was killed, she began collecting books written by people who'd reported near-death experiences and, by their account, had seen a glimpse of Heaven. She explained to me that she wasn't sure if she believed everything the authors wrote, but she read the books because she wanted to know where Todd was—she wanted to be able to close her eyes and picture it. And besides that, she couldn't wait to go there one day. I like to imagine where she is now, and most of the time, I can't stretch my mind enough to picture it. So I live in a state of gratitude that my life was touched by Nan, and I honor her by revisiting all the crazy, goofy, lovely things that made her unique.

(And I continue to crack up every time I see an electric back massager.)

Country Life

Anything for a Date

My strapping husband and I had been married for a year and a half, and one Saturday in late March, I was dying to go out on a date. Our baby girl, Alex, was a few months old, and I was still neck deep in the adjustment phase that had included (in no particular order) marriage, motherhood, and moving to the middle of nowhere. For the first eighteen months of our newlywed stage, Ladd and I (and now, our child) had been in you-and-me-against-the-world mode, living in our little house on the prairie and trying to weather the various storms (financial stress and my parents' divorce, to name a couple) that had befallen us during that time. We hadn't had much social interaction with others, as it seemed like we were just trying to get our bearings all the time. But by golly, on that particular night we'd been officially invited out to dinner with some couples in Pawhuska—and I was *ready*.

Ladd, on the other hand, was not. He was exhausted, having had a backbreaking week of work on the ranch, and all he wanted to do was strip off his muddy clothes, take a twenty-minute shower, and settle in for the evening with his quiet little family. "How about if I take you out tomorrow night," he suggested. "I don't have to work tomorrow, so we can leave earlier in the day and go see a movie."

But I didn't want to see a movie. I wanted to put on slim black pants, a sleek shirt, and high-heeled boots, then go to a restaurant in the city with some other married couples. I wanted to wear red lipstick, have adult conversation, and be witty. As much as I loved my husband, we were alone together all the time. I wanted to spend the evening having cocktails with new friends while flipping my hair and laughing. It had to happen that night or we might never have the chance again for the rest of our lives.

I was in the middle of pleading my case to Ladd, possibly stomping my feet a little, when he looked away and suddenly ran into our bedroom. I thought this was a bit of an overreaction to my asking to go out with other couples, but he *had* just had a long day, I reminded myself. Seconds later, though, he emerged from the bedroom wielding a shotgun and ran with lightning speed toward the front door . . . and when I looked outside the window at our yard, I instantly understood what was going on: The skunk was running toward our house.

A bit of background: At our little house on the prairie, we had a skunk problem. On a pretty continual basis, except for the coldest months of winter, skunks had decided they liked it under our house, and it made our lives a stinky hell. They scratched their backs on nails and boards, and it was actually as if I was burning a Skunk Essence candle when they were down there doing their thing. Skunk smell when you're driving down the highway is one thing; skunk smell wafting up into your marital home on a daily basis is quite another. Those were some pretty dark, disgusting days.

In recent weeks, we'd had enough, and had been weeding out the skunks one by one by fashioning a board to cover the breach that the skunks were using to get in and out, occasionally blocking the hole with the board anytime we saw a skunk scurrying away from the house, presumably to go hunt and forage. The idea was that when they came back (whatever time of day that would be), the inn would be closed and they'd move on to greener pastures. Of course, it also meant trapping some skunks under the house for hours at a time—but we had a system, albeit a clunky one, and it had been working. It was a long, painstaking process that required patience and some lucky timing, but sure enough, by now almost all of them were gone . . . that is, except for the lone skunk ranger. He'd been completely elusive, sneaking in and out for weeks, and we never seemed to be able to catch him, whether coming or going. Earlier that morning, as we'd done regularly, we removed the board, hoping we'd catch him coming out but doubtful we'd be that lucky.

So now, in the late afternoon, after Ladd's long day of work and before the date he didn't want to go on, there he was! The elusive skunk was finally in our sight. He'd obviously left our house without our knowing earlier in the day, and at this moment he was running at full skunk speed back to his dark little den, also known as our home. Ladd saw him and knew the board was still off the house, and that this was his one chance to make sure our skunk days were forever behind us. And so, about fifteen feet from our house . . . *BOOM!* The skunk was no longer an issue, and a pungent, greenish mist hovered in the air. Ladd immediately secured the board to the base of the house, then put the shotgun back in its place. Victory was ours. Our skunk problem was solved. Now I really had a reason to celebrate with new friends that night!

Ladd, however, was still trying to wriggle out of

it. "Aw, let's stay home," he said, taking off his boots. "We'll pop popcorn and watch movies."

"But I want to get out in the world," I pouted. "I'm going to shrivel and die if I don't go out tonight."

"I'm going to shrivel and die if I go," he countered. Clever boy.

"I'm going to shrivel and die and *cry*," I said. Even cleverer girl.

That got him where it hurt. Ladd was unnerved by crying. It stumped him. But he wasn't going down without a fight, and he pulled out all the stops: "Tell ya what," he said with a smirk. "You get the dead skunk out of the yard while I go shower, and we'll go out with all those guys tonight." Then he walked in the bathroom and turned on the shower, probably patting himself on the back over his coup.

The gauntlet was thrown. Alex by now was awake from her nap, so I put her in her bouncy seat and did something I never imagined, in my wildest childhood or teenage dreams, I would do in my life: I went outside with a black trash bag, wearing Ladd's work gloves. I dug around in his toolbox in the back of his pickup and found huge pliers, then walked slowly and purposefully over to the dead skunk. Holding the pliers in my right gloved hand, I reached all the way to the bottom of the empty bag, used the pliers to grab hold of the skunk's leg from inside of the bag . . . then lifted it up and inverted the trash bag over the body. I sealed the bag and stood there, not even sure how in the world I'd come up with that method.

But it didn't matter: I did it! I got the dead skunk out of the yard. And it was done before Ladd was even out of the shower.

When he turned off the water and came out of the bathroom, I directed his attention to the empty spot in the yard where the skunk had been. He looked at me with shock, shook his head, tried not to smile, and said, "Crap . . ." He would never have guessed I'd be capable of getting that close to a wild animal, let alone allowing myself to touch it. (I neglected to tell him I hadn't actually touched it. I wanted to keep my methods to myself.) Tail between his legs, my husband skulked into the bedroom to get dressed for our hot date.

I had officially won. I was sorry about the skunk's abrupt end, but it's a harsh reality of country life that sometimes man and wildlife have to go toe to toe in turf wars such as these. As for me, I'd pushed through and, by sheer will, had taken on Ladd's challenge. I'd completely called his bluff. I was ready for our date! I got dressed up and we dropped Alex at my mother-in-law's house, then met the group of couples in town, where we loaded up in a couple of SUVs for the hour-long drive to the restaurant.

Once we were all in our seats and buckled in, one of the ladies looked around and said, "Whew! What is that *smell?*"

I guess the skunk made sure he got the last word.

I Really Hate Summer

Growing up a freckled, fun-loving child who lived just a hop, a skip, and a jump from the country club pool, I always thought summer was the happiest time of year. From as young as I can remember, my daily schedule in the summertime began with zero urgency, at whatever time my natural clock told me to roll out of bed. Breakfast consisted of either bacon and eggs cooked by my mom or a big bowl of Cocoa Puffs, whichever struck my fancy. Then I'd get cleaned up and head to the pool, where I'd meet up with my very best friend, Becky. The two of us would stay there until the sun started to go down (we must have been handfuls, because our moms never sent for us), spending all our time giggling, playing Marco Polo, buying grilled cheeses and frozen Snickers from the snack bar, and laying out. Summer was easy, summer was beautiful, summer was free.

Many years later, after I'd gone to college in California, eaten my fill of sushi, dated a surfer, and moved back to Oklahoma, I became engaged to Ladd, a cowboy from the next county. Before we got married, I enjoyed getting acquainted with his mother, Nan, my future mother-in-law, who doled out random pieces of advice regarding my upcoming future as an agricultural wife and rural resident, a fate I'd never imagined for myself. I lapped up every word she had to say. It was all so very interesting! Among her practical tips for country living were things like buying multiples of grocery items, investing in a larger-than-normal upright freezer, planting flowers that could withstand harsh winds and hail, painting our homestead a natural color so enemies flying overhead couldn't spot us (see page 214), and never walking outside at night without shoes. I listened and took it all in—especially when she uttered a phrase I'd never heard before. It was a phrase so foreign in concept, in fact, that I could hardly grasp the idea.

"And one more thing," Nan said, peering over her glasses. "Get ready to really hate summer."

Hate . . . summer? "Huh?" I replied. "I don't understand."

"You will," she said, before moving on to pantry-stocking tips. I was a little confused, but decided to tuck it away in a tiny recess of my brain in case it ever came up.

Fast-forward a quarter of a century: I really hate summer, just like Nan said I would. And let me tell you why.

Forget feeding cattle and chopping icy ponds in the winter. On a ranch, summer is when the *real* work begins. First, Ladd and his brother have to get all the cattle ready for the summer grass. They have to worm the cattle, give them all their vaccinations, work all the spring calves, and preg test all the cows (that's short for "pregnancy test," but they do it so often that we decided to save them a couple of syllables). And as soon as they get all of that marked off the list, they've got to start cutting, baling, hauling, and putting up hay, which is a solid three-week ordeal. Before the final bales even make it to the stackyard, they have to start shipping cattle, which lasts for another few weeks. So basically, there are six or seven major summer tasks that overlap one another, and the kicker is this: All of it (with the exception of hay) has to be done early in the morning, before it gets too hot. Avoiding working in the brutal afternoon sun is better for the cowboys, it's better for the cattle, and it's better for the pocketbook (because the cattle don't lose weight by sweating).

This all means that for a big chunk of the summer, we often have to get our rear ends out of bed at 3:45 in the morning. And I don't know about you, but where I come from, 3:45 in the morning isn't actually the morning. It's the middle of the night.

Getting up this early as an individual human is difficult enough, but it's particularly dicey with four children, especially when the children's father had to get up at 3:45 a.m. in the summer during *his* childhood and by golly, his kids aren't gonna be slackers! There is no pool life for my kids. There isn't even lake life. The kids all have to go work, too, just like their dad, and as much as I would love to roll over and put a pillow over my head while they get up and head out into the darkness, I am afflicted with ranch wife syndrome and feel that I also must get up and suffer with them. When the kids were little, I had to help them gather their clothes, round up their boots, find their spurs, and remind them to brush their teeth. Now that they are teenagers, I have to physically pull them out of bed because of their adolescent comas.

Let me repeat: 3:45 a.m. is the middle of the night.

In May and even June, this summer schedule is

hard. But by July and August, it becomes downright unbearable. Sunday is really the only day that's safe, as we take the "day of rest" concept seriously—beyond that, depending on the week, we can find ourselves getting up at 3:45 a.m. for six days in a row. It is unrelenting and crazy-making, and it causes me to question everything. I lose my REM sleep. I lose my looks. I lose hope. I get cranky. I try to stay on top of my own work and projects, but as soon as I get any momentum, the family gets home, exhausted, and I have to wash their jeans before the mud and manure become permanently bonded to the threads of the denim. Then I make lunch. Then they nap. And before I know it, it's 10:00 p.m. and all I have to look forward to is my alarm going off (or my husband poking me in the rib cage) less than six hours later.

What I'm getting at is that I'm not sure how much longer I can do this. Summer will eventually break me. And this is exactly what I try to tell my husband during our typical early-morning/middle-of-the-night 3:45 a.m. exchanges, when Ladd wakes me up to tell me it's time to wake up the kids. He's already halfway dressed and has to go start saddling the horses, which can take up to thirty minutes. So I'm on kid wake-up duty. The routine goes something like this:

"Honey," he says tenderly, touching my shoulder.

I don't move.

"Honey," he tries again.

"Mmmrfppph." I sniff, snort, and pretend I don't hear him.

"Hey, honey," he says, not so tenderly poking my shoulder this time.

I jerk away from him in protest, as if he's startled me from a nightmare. "No," I mumble, pulling the quilt over my head and squeezing it tightly so as to close off all access from the outside world.

"Mama," he says, poking my ribs through the quilt. He doesn't even have to see my ribs. After twenty-four years, he knows exactly where they are.

"*NOOOOOOOOOO-wuhhhhh . . .*" I groan. I sound like an irritated teenager.

"Get up, get up, you sleepyhead," Ladd sings—and very off tune. It's one of the few things he can't do well. I want to punch him and cry at the same time. And I'm normally not the punching, crying type.

"Fine . . . ," I say, trying to blink my eyes into staying open. "But I need to tell you something."

"What's that?" he asks, buttoning his jeans and finally confirming that I am, in fact, awake.

"I want a divorce," I tell him plainly. Communication is the key in any healthy relationship, after all.

"Tell the kids to wear their chaps," he replies as he

buckles his belt. "It rained last night and it's gonna be muddy."

"It still is last night!" I insist. "And I can't do this another day. I'm losing my religion and my mind. I have ceased to exist and dream. I can no longer create and thrive. Give the girls my grandmother's china, please. Tell the boys I love them."

He leans over me and pokes my ribs again. "You're funny," he says, chuckling. We've had this same conversation since 2003.

And anyway, he has to head down to the barn. There are horses to round up and saddle. He doesn't want to be late meeting the other cowboys. So I roll out of bed and wake up the kids, then go pour them all an orange juice before searching for wayward socks, boots, jeans, chaps, shirts, spurs, and hats. I walk with them down to the barn and make sure everyone is good before waving as they drive off with their dad and the five-horse trailer. Then I stumble back in the house and knock out my first big chore of the day: sitting down with a large glass of cold-brew coffee mixed with a little sweetened condensed milk and finished with a splash of cream. The first sip ensures my survival.

I guess divorce can wait till tomorrow.

Gardening Heartbreak

I never gardened before I married Ladd, but once I moved to the country and was bitten by the bug, I fell madly in love. Once I really found my green thumb, I felt like a redheaded Mother Earth, hauling loamy dirt from the river bottom to mix with the clayey soil at our house and planting zucchini, tomatoes, cucumbers, melons, peppers, potatoes, and all the herbs God has bestowed upon the earth. I did this partly because I love garden-fresh vegetables, but mostly because I loved staring at my garden and experiencing that self-congratulatory feeling of horticultural accomplishment. Also, it made me feel like a complete stud. Or whatever the female word for "stud" is. (Does such a word even exist?) Still, with gardening always comes a certain measure of heartbreak, and it seems like the measure I was given was a little bigger than others'.

In addition to veggies, I also grew flowers around my house, because flowers give my soul something to live for. I was the only girl in my sorority who wore bright floral Adrienne Vittadini outfits from head to toe; everyone else was rocking sleek Guess jeans and black leather jackets, like normal college girls. When Ladd and I moved to the homestead where we live now, it was almost completely flowerless. So, lest my psyche start to shrivel, I planted zinnias, huge Russian sage, salvia, echinacea, rudbeckia, gaillardia . . . all the beautiful flowers that thrive in Oklahoma's extreme wind and blistering heat. Oh, and I planted roses. Lots and lots of roses.

One variety of rose I became especially enamored with was named "Hot Cocoa" for the deep, rich shade of brownish-red petals. The color was stunning, but so was the shape of the blooms—and after I successfully grew a gorgeous bush one summer, the following spring I planted eleven more. They were a triumph, and the foundation of all the decorative vegetation around my front porch. Over the following year, my Hot Cocoa roses grew gorgeous and thick, and my gardening pride was at an all-time high.

But one day, to my great dismay, one of the Hot Cocoa rosebushes started failing. It slowly lost its parchmentlike blooms, then quit flowering altogether.

I tried special rose food and fertilizer, as well as pesticide and fungicide, but soon the leaves started dropping off, and within three weeks, it was completely dead. Meanwhile, the other eleven Hot Cocoa bushes were absolutely thriving, with no sign of disease at all. I was completely puzzled, and I hated the idea of starting a young new bush from scratch. It had taken a year to get these all to full glory. The dead bush left a hole in my landscaping and in my heart.

A few evenings later, I found out the cause. It was accidental but fortuitous. I happened to walk by a window at the front of our house just in time to see Ladd peeing off the porch . . . *right in the spot of the deceased rosebush.* And it's not like I didn't know Ladd peed outside. He does it, the cowboys do it, my boys do it—just like millennia of country boys have done before. It saves water and it's convenient . . . and let's face it, there are no neighbors to see it happening. But it hadn't once occurred to me that any peeing was taking place off the porch, let alone on my flowers, let alone on one of my prized Hot Cocoa rosebushes. But there was my answer. My poor, beloved plant had experienced death by urine, also known as nitrogen burn. To put it bluntly: Ladd had killed my rosebush by peeing on it repeatedly. If that doesn't sum up everything that's wrong with country boys, I don't know what does.

I whipped open the front door, shrieked, "What are you *doing*?!?" and startled Ladd so badly that he told me he couldn't pee anymore. Which was good, I replied, because if he couldn't start being more responsible about his pee, it wasn't something he needed to be doing anyway.

Back to the vegetable world for a second. Did I ever tell you my cherry tomato story?

Growing tomatoes in Oklahoma is a no-brainer, and they're always the main focus of my garden. They love nothing more than hot, full sun in the summertime, and we have that in abundance in my state. Back in my tomato heyday years ago, I was always happiest when I had an eclectic variety of tomato plants, so I made it a point to plant beefsteaks, heirlooms, big boys, steakhouses—in all the colors you can imagine.

I always grew tomatoes from starter plants that I sometimes ordered but usually bought at local garden spots. I never grew them from seeds, because when it comes to tomatoes I'm impatient and always want to get the show on the road as fast as possible. One summer I bought all my tomato plants in one go, to save time, and hauled them back to the ranch to start planting. I should also mention that this particular year, I was extra excited for spring, so I went overboard and got almost twice as many tomato plants as I'd bought the year before. I pictured entertaining for friends and setting out big white platters of tomato slices in gorgeous shades of yellow, red, maroon, and brown. I could almost hear their oohs and aahs, and the tomatoes hadn't even started growing yet. I couldn't wait to show off my bounty!

When the plants started bearing fruit, I discovered to my (relative) horror that every single tomato plant in my garden was growing . . . cherry tomatoes. All of them. Every single one. Evidently, wherever they'd originated, an employee had gotten distracted and mislabeled an entire truckload of tomato plants. Bottom line, I harvested approximately 12,098,234,151,223 cherry tomatoes that summer, and it was many, many years before I could eat them again. Have you ever tried to fill big white platters with sliced cherry tomatoes?

It takes a while. A good, sharp knife is recommended.

If you've ever grown a sunflower—and many elementary school children in America have—you understand the wonder of watching a single seed grow into a stalk that's six or seven feet tall (sometimes more), and finally develop the big, beautiful bloom on top. They're absolute happiness in the form of a plant, and one summer, to give me and my vegetable garden a rest, I decided to plant nothing but different heights, sizes, and colors of sunflowers.

I researched the varieties and mail-ordered the seeds, then planted them in stages so that the entire garden, the tall and the short, would be in full bloom at the exact same time. I waited. And watered. (And enjoyed not maintaining my veggie garden that year. Mama needed a break after that cherry tomato saga.)

The location for the sunflower garden was perfect—away from the house a little ways and protected by an old rock wall that was built around the perimeter of our house back in the 1930s. The textured sandstone was the perfect backdrop for the growing sunflowers, and every day I got such joy from watching the plants get closer and closer to maturity. And it seems like it truly did happen overnight; out of the blue, sunflowers opened up and revealed their gorgeousness left and right. Some blooms were as small as appetizer plates; others were as large as dinner plates. My dream—my sunflowers—had finally arrived! It was real! I made plans to photograph the garden the next morning as the sun was rising in the east, and imagined the dreamy photos I could take with my kids skipping through the stalks.

I headed outside the next morning with my camera and noticed a gorgeous light fog, which was sure to provide the perfect vibe for an entire album's worth of garden portraits. But when I turned the corner and caught a glimpse, I discovered that my sunflower garden was completely missing its blooms, except for the five small plants in the very front row. The rest of the stalks— around sixty of them, some as tall as eight feet—just stood there, waving gently in the morning breeze like skinny green headless horsemen. My knees went weak. My *sunflowers*! They were gone, faster than presents are opened on Christmas morning. My throat started to swell a little.

I heard a rustle in the back, so I walked around to the edge of the garden and looked on the other side of the rock wall. Our seven ranch horses—Snip, L.B., Red, Pepper, Peso, Old Yeller, and Jack—all stood there staring at me, chomping on what I immediately realized were the very last bites of the most luxuriant breakfast they'd probably ever had: an entire buffet of my long-awaited sunflower blooms. In my years of gardening, I'd never experienced the horses eating anything I'd grown—they don't like the taste of tomato plants, and that alone kept them away from my veggies. So I had a false sense of security with the sunflowers. I'd just wasted nearly three months of my life growing the equine buttheads one single, enormous meal.

I think the sunflower garden incident was my most heartbreaking garden heartbreak of all, because not only did I lose my sunflowers in one fell swoop, they disappeared at the hands (mouths) of my now-ex equine friends. I secretly hoped they'd all get a two-day belly-ache after their gluttonous stunt, but nothing. In fact, their coats were especially shiny for the next couple of weeks.

Today I'm back to planting vegetables, and I just admire sunflowers from afar. I can't ever let myself be hurt like that again.

Horses on Drummond Ranch

— Neigh

Despite their tendency to eat my sunflowers,
horses are a huge part of our family, and they have
really cute names. Here are some loyal fellas
who've carried Ladd, Tim, the cowboys, and the kids
through the years. Some are no longer with us,
some still report for duty every day. There's nothing
like the love of a good ranch horse!

* Old Yeller
* Snip
* Jack
* L.B.
* Buddy
* Peso
* Pokey
* Flash
* Ford
* Cutter
* Pepper
* Red
* Goose
* Zero

* Mighty Mouse
* Lizard
* Sheldon
* Tigger
* Joey
* Peanut
* Moonshine
* Little Bit
* Batman
* Beemer
* Shooter
* Buster
* Bubba
* Church

Shopping in Bulk

Growing up in a normal town, within normal distance of grocery and other types of stores, I learned the practice of shopping for things as they're needed. Oh, I guess my mom would stock up a little bit when she'd go to the grocery store—for instance, she might shop on Monday for the rest of the week's groceries. Or toward the end of summer, we'd buy school supplies for the year. Or before the weather got cold, we'd buy a couple of sweaters and maybe a new coat. But generally speaking, I enjoyed the luxury of being able to run to the supermarket, the pharmacy, the clothing store as needed, for the first twenty-five-plus years of my life.

When I married Ladd and moved to the country, I was still conditioned in this way, and probably a little worse: I'd gone to school in California and lived alone there for long enough that I'd become accustomed to shopping each day for that evening's dinner. So for the first few months of my marriage to Ladd, I took that same approach—which was taxing considering we lived many miles from town and I had morning sickness because of something that happened on our honeymoon. So, for example, I'd drive to town and grab some chicken breasts, pasta, and the makings for a simple sauce, then I'd drive back home, completely nauseated at the idea that I had raw poultry in my vehicle. Then I'd do it again the next day, and it wouldn't go any more smoothly.

Bless Ladd's heart, now that I think about it, because he would make subtle suggestions to me like "If you make a list of what you need, I'll go to Ponca City and get a big load" and "We can go to the store together on Saturday if you make your list." For the life of me, I couldn't figure out what he meant. He was describing, of course, buying in bulk—taking one big trip to the store to get many weeks' worth of supplies—which was the way he'd always seen it done growing up. But at the time, the idea of filling an entire vehicle (even sometimes a horse trailer) with groceries was a foreign concept.

Nan, my mother-in-law, began to teach me the ropes. She excelled at bulk buying and approached it with all the pragmatism of a home economics major: Why buy one pack of diapers on multiple drives to the supermarket an hour away when I could buy fifteen packs of diapers on just one supermarket visit? Why buy a pound of butter in each of twenty trips when I could buy twenty pounds in one trip? The math, the gas savings, and the time savings (not to mention the decreased wear and tear on the tires and on me) just made sense. Nan had a lot of experience in this department.

In the early days on the ranch, during the first few years Chuck and Nan were married, there had definitely been a feast-or-famine quality to the cash flow. Cattle were sold once or twice a year, which meant that all the household income flowed into the bank on one or two (very blessed) days annually. Credit cards weren't a big thing, and interest rates were high, which made borrowing money during the drier months possible but never ideal. So Nan learned quickly that when the cattle were sold, it was time for her to get what she needed—because if she waited too long, Chuck would buy a tractor or make a down payment on another parcel of land, and the cash would start to get low. She'd make a huge trip to the city for nonperishable (and freezable) supplies that would last her many months—then just fill in her perishables (milk, eggs, bread) as needed at the local grocery store in town.

It carried over into the non-food world as well. When Chuck sold the ranch's cattle, Nan would go shopping for clothing for her three sons—enough to last for months or more. She'd hit the department stores and sometimes come out with twenty-five pairs of jeans (for three sons plus Chuck), forty work shirts, fifty pairs of socks, and more underwear than some stores even stocked. She was swift, merciless, and full of purpose. She told me that once, on a post-cattle-sale shopping day, she bit off more than she could chew and had to call Chuck from Tulsa and have him make the hour-and-a-half drive to pick up some of her purchases.

Ironically, Nan was not a shopaholic. This bulk-buying practice was in no way reflective of materialism or hoarding on her part; she simply knew that she had few ideal windows in which to get the things she would need for her ranching family for a several-month period, and instead of pacing them out over the normal span of a year, she'd get in there and get 'er done.

The complication came later, when Nan's boys were grown and out of the house. Christmas would roll around, and when Ladd opened a gift from her, inside the box would be nine shirts. If she found a night cream she liked, she had a hard time not buying eight jars. It took years for her to break the habit of stocking her pantry, bathroom shelves, and closet with multiples.

So this was my bulk-buying mentor: Nan, the bulk-buying queen herself. Under her tutelage and influence, I became a pro at making very infrequent trips to the supermarket and the discount club. It was less about cash flow, as times were different in ranching, and operating on a line of credit from the bank (interest rates are better now) mitigated the feast-or-famine phenomenon Nan had experienced. But it was very much about making the decision not to spend my life in the car, driving hours a day with four babies and coming back with only a week or two's worth of supplies to show for it. So I became a scholar. I learned quickly and became entirely comfortable with buying dozens of bars of soap at a time. And don't get me started on canned tomatoes. Dozens were not enough.

After a while, though, times started to change. Online shopping became more prevalent, and because the kids became involved in different sports (some through a homeschooling league in the big city), I found myself having to leave the ranch more and more anyway. So I never became the full-blown, necessity-based bulk buyer that Nan was in the old days of the ranch. And besides that, an incident happened early on that had dampened my enthusiasm.

I'd made the trek to Walmart, two of my four kids in tow, and spent two exhausting hours going up and down every aisle, ticking off my list until I'd filled four—yes, four—large carts. I was very proud of the work I'd done, and the carts were orderly and organized according to category: dry goods, clothing, toiletries, housecleaning products, storage and paper goods, and perishables. The four carts were mounded and bulging, and as I lined them up in the checkout lane, a man in the next aisle looked in my direction. As I started emptying the cart full of toiletries, he stared at my eight twelve-packs of Dove soap and said, very loudly, "Dang, lady! Are you one of them shopaholics? You a spendthrift or somethin'?"

"No," I answered. "I . . ."

I wanted to explain the whole thing—that we live out in the country, and that it is a much more efficient use of time and resources for me to do fewer shopping trips a year. That I'm married to a busy cattle rancher and raising four kids, and there are hardly enough hours in the day if I stay home 24-7, let alone drive up and down the road all the time, and the fewer treks I can make to the city, the more sane a person I'll be. Plus, my mother-in-law said so! You should listen to her, sir!!! I decided I wasn't comfortable with that kind of attention, especially in the checkout line.

"I'm . . . buying it for my church," I lied, blinking coyly and flashing him an angelic smile.

(I hope God didn't mind too much.)

Stockin' Up

Even though I'm no longer deep in the bulk-buying years, I still love having a well-stocked kitchen in case something crazy like a zombie apocalypse (or a pandemic) happens and I can't get to civilization for supplies. Here's my working list!

PANTRY

Baking

* Baking ingredients: bulk flour (all-purpose, whole wheat, cake, self-rising), sugar, brown sugar, powdered sugar, baking powder, baking soda, yeast, cream of tartar
* Chocolate chips, cocoa powder, and other kinds of baking chocolate
* Evaporated milk and sweetened condensed milk
* Shortening

Canned and Jarred

* Artichoke hearts: throw in a pasta sauce, make artichoke dip, or put on pizza
* Assorted olives, jalapeños, pepperoncini
* Canned beans: great for salads and soups. Rinse before adding!

* Canned tomatoes: crushed, whole, diced, stewed, paste
* Chipotle peppers in adobo sauce: add to soups and roasts, mix with mayo, add to dip
* Jarred pesto and specialty relishes and chutneys
* Jellies: strawberry, apricot, jalapeño
* Peanut butter
* Roasted red peppers: place them on panini, puree and make a soup or pasta sauce, chop for bruschetta
* Ro*tel canned tomatoes with green chilies
* Stocks and broths: chicken, beef, vegetable

Condiments, Flavorings, Herbs, and Spices

* Barbecue sauce
* Dried herbs and spices
* Honey
* Hot sauce
* Ketchup, different mustards, relish
* Maple syrup, pancake syrup
* Mayonnaise
* Olive oil, vegetable oil, peanut oil, coconut oil
* Rice wine (mirin)
* Salt: iodized, kosher, sea salt, salt blends
* Soy sauce, fish sauce, teriyaki sauce, hoisin
* Vinegars: distilled white, red wine, white wine, apple cider, rice wine
* Worcestershire

Boxed and packaged

* Cornmeal
* Dried beans: pinto, black, Great Northern, navy
* Dried pasta in every shape and size
* Oatmeal and other breakfast grains
* Masa: corn flour, sold in the Hispanic foods aisle; use to make tortillas, add to chili
* Panko breadcrumbs: top casseroles, coat fried mozzarella, mix into meatballs
* Rice: long grain, brown, jasmine, Arborio

Vegetables

* Potatoes, onions, and garlic: store them in a basket so air can circulate

FRIDGE

* Bacon
* Butter by the ton!
* Cheese: long-lasting varieties like Cheddar, Parmesan, feta
* Eggs
* Heavy cream: for cooking, desserts, and coffee
* Lemons, limes, apples, carrots, celery
* Tortillas: flour and corn; if stored properly, they seem to last forever in the fridge

(NOTE: The fridge list contains only long-lasting staples. Fill in the more perishable items weekly or biweekly!)

FREEZER

* Beef, wrapped in butcher paper
* Bread: crusty artisan loaves, sandwich breads
* Chicken: breasts, wings, legs, thighs
* Frozen dinner rolls (unbaked): make them as rolls or use them for calzones or hand pies
* Frozen fruits: pineapple, berries, mango. Great for smoothies, pies, crisps, cobblers
* Frozen vegetables: peas, corn, butternut squash, broccoli, green beans
* Nuts such as pecans, walnuts, almonds: keeps them from going rancid
* Pie crust
* Pizza dough
* Raw shrimp
* Sausage: breakfast sausage, Italian sausage, chorizo

Bull, Interrupted

On a cattle ranch, male calves (also called bull calves) are typically castrated when they're very young. Once castrated, they become steers, which are the kind of animal typically sold on the beef market. (Female calves, also known as heifers, can also eventually be sold as beef—or they can be added to a cow herd for breeding purposes.) There are many reasons to castrate a bull calf: it halts the production of testosterone, thereby making the animal less aggressive; and it causes the animal to have less muscle mass, which results in higher-quality, more tender beef. Castrating is just a regular part of animal management in a cattle operation.

Calf nuts, at certain times of year, are everywhere on the ranch. I remember Ladd asking me to stop by my in-laws' house early in our marriage to grab a couple of packages of home-grown ground beef from their freezer. They were out of town, so I let myself in the back door and casually swung open the freezer door. Along with packages of ground beef, there was shelf after shelf of plastic freezer bags, bulging with frightening-looking oval-shaped objects I couldn't recognize at all. There were veins and membranes visible under the surface of the frozen ovals, and I immediately slammed the door and ran out of the house, telling Ladd when I got home that his parents didn't have any ground beef. I lied, but I had to. Whatever was in my father-in-law's freezer scared the life out of me. I later came to understand that they were calf nuts. And hundreds of them.

Many country people eat calf nuts—partly because it's a shame to let them go to waste, but also because some consider them to be a delicacy. They are typically prepared like fried chicken—breaded and deep-fried—and entire "calf fry" dinners are held (usually after a bunch of calves have been processed) wherein batch after batch of calf nuts are cooked in an outdoor turkey fryer and enjoyed fresh as they come out of the oil. (Dipping sauces are optional for some, absolutely required for me.) My brother-in-law Tim is known for his delicious nuts (sorry, I'm five years old and am laughing so hard as I write this) . . . I mean, for the delicious manner in which he prepares fried calf nuts. His secret is cutting them into pretty small pieces—picture a bite-size chicken nugget—and generously seasoning the flour with salt, pepper, and lots of cayenne.

I suppose if I had to eat calf nuts every day for the rest of my life, I would choose Tim's version . . . but I would be a pretty unhappy person, because I simply do not like them. And I guess I want to like them. After all, I'm considered one of the more adventurous eaters in the Drummond family! But there's something about them that trips me up, and I believe it's a mind-over-matter scenario. I'll pop one in my mouth, chew a couple of times, and start to think whatever I'm eating is pretty tasty—but then the reality of what I'm eating kicks in, and within seconds I'm sorry I ate it. I've actually spit one or two out before, because my mind attacks me and forces me to. I won't ever judge anyone for eating calf nuts (or Rocky Mountain oysters, as they're euphemistically called in some restaurants), as I think it's responsible to use as much of the animals as we can for food. But it's way down at about #2,985 on the list of things I crave on any given day.

The food component aside, there's a strange peripheral issue that comes up during the times on the ranch when calves are being castrated. Without giving too technical of a rundown, on our ranch we castrate the calves surgically, using a sharp pocketknife. (Other methods involve banding or clamping, but we prefer the fast way. It's over much sooner for the little guys!) The whole castration process takes about eighteen seconds per calf, and the first step of it involves slicing around and removing the fuzzy, fatty skin that's covering the testicles. It comes off looking very similar to a rabbit's foot, only much softer and cuter—and by the end of a busy morning of working calves, we might have a pile of a hundred or more of them on the ground. (I won't go into the actual castration process, but it's a very simple tug/slice and then it's over.)

The weirdness comes into play because these little furry coverings are incredibly soft, *and* incredibly interesting from a texture standpoint. Because of this, they attract the attention of any kids that are on-site, and throughout the course of the morning, it isn't unusual to see the kids picking up the little sacs and holding them, fiddling with them, playing with them, and—here's the kicker—putting them in their pockets, which means they inadvertently forget and leave them there, which means they invariably wind up in the washer and dryer.

In case this will help any parents out there who contribute to the laundry duties of the household: If you don't already check your children's jeans pockets before you throw them in the washing machine, please do so—especially if you live in the country, and especially if you live on a working cattle ranch. Because the odor that results from not only washing, but also drying, the fuzzy sac that covers a calf's testicles is not something your laundry room—or your sinuses—will ever forget.

This has been a public service announcement.

The Lodge Tourists

A year or so after we opened our restaurant and store in Pawhuska, Ladd suggested it might be nice to start opening up the Lodge, our guesthouse on the ranch where we film my Food Network show, for free tours when it isn't being used for filming. The Lodge largely sits empty when we aren't shooting my show or having some kind of family event, and in his way of thinking, offering folks a chance to drive out and walk around (and take in the view, which is stunning from the Lodge) would only serve to expand their visit to Pawhuska and give them more bang for their buck. I thought it sounded like a promising idea but told Ladd I needed a couple of weeks to think over the pros and cons, to which he responded, "Okay, but let's go ahead and start tours tomorrow." When my husband gets a notion in his head, he sees no reason to think over anything. Fortunately, most of his ideas are good.

Lodge tours did, in fact, start the next day, and have been going strong for the past three years. We have a couple of employees there on Lodge tour days, and they answer questions about the area and invite people to browse freely, check out the various rooms, and (yes, I really don't mind) peek inside the drawers. To our surprise, the Lodge has actually become an attraction all its own, with folks sometimes returning to Pawhuska just to take another drive to the ranch and bring a new family member with them. It's always fun to walk through an actual place you've seen on TV, so I totally understand the fun of it. I would be over the moon, for example, to visit Coto de Caza, the gated community in *The Real Housewives of Orange County*. But maybe that's just me.

Sometimes people hear that we open our home to visitors and have lots of questions for us. "How can you let strangers into your home?" they say, confused. "How does that even work?" But the truth is, while the Lodge is Ladd's and my home, it's a guesthouse on the ranch and isn't where we live and lay our heads at night. And in fact, the road that leads to the Lodge is a good mile and a half past the road that leads to our house, so it's really like two parallel worlds are existing: everyday life at my house, where teenage boy underwear litters the floor and cow manure litters the yard . . . and everyday life at the Lodge, where there's no dirty laundry or cow manure anywhere, just a gorgeous view of open rangeland and a cool kitchen some people recognize from TV. So Lodge tours can go on happily without our intersecting with them too much, and it's turned out to be a pretty great thing—good job, Ladd! Only three or four times has a Lodge tourist misread directions and wound up on our road instead, and they usually realize it and turn around before they arrive at our house.

A few months ago, at about four in the afternoon, I decided, quite uncharacteristically, to take a bath. I'd been on a long walk and was sweaty and gross, and Ladd and the boys were out of town working cattle in Kansas. It was the perfect time to have a rare Calgon moment, so I used all the bubble bath I could get my hands on and settled in, using my toes to occasionally turn the faucet and add more hot water to the mix. I had a good hour before the guys would be home, and life was good.

I was naked, submerged, and almost half asleep when I heard pounding on the front door. It startled me, as I obviously wasn't expecting anyone, and I just stayed in the bathtub. There was no way I could hop out, manage not to slip and fall, and put on a robe in time to get to the front door and answer it . . . and even then, who knows who it would be? What if it was a serial killer? I mean, it's possible.

The pounding happened again. My phone wasn't even in my room, and worse, the full-size window next to my bathtub looks out onto the front porch . . . and is covered with extremely sheer curtains. (We don't have neighbors, remember.) Any movement on my part would have been detected by whoever was pounding on the front door, and then, not only would they know I was home, they would also see me naked, which I hadn't signed up for that afternoon. I truly had no choice but to lie there perfectly still, a prisoner in my own bathtub.

I heard the faint sounds of chatter among two or three women; I couldn't make out what they were saying, but it did seem like they might be about to give up and head out. But then, to my surprise, our door alarm chimed, indicating that someone had opened it. "Hello?!?" a woman's voice called out, echoing in the living room. "Hello?!? Is anyone here?!?" I heard more chatter among the unexpected visitors.

"Hello?!?" another woman's voice called out, even more loudly. It overlapped with the first one. I was still frozen in the hot bathtub, having not a clue what to do. All I knew was that I was in no condition or mood to encounter humans that weren't my husband or boys. And there were unfamiliar strangers in my house—not on my porch, but in my house. And I was naked. So very, very naked. More naked than I'd ever been! And did I mention my bedroom door was wide open?

There were more "Hello?!?" cries, and then I listened carefully to try to hear their conversation.

"I know this is the place," one voice said.

"It has to be," another said. "Look, there are her cookbooks." I had a stack of cookbooks in my kitchen; I was going to sign them for some donations later that evening after my bath. The bath that I was still being held captive in, by the way.

Then I heard a third voice. "There's literally nobody here," she said. "Should we just take the tour anyway?"

They thought they were at the Lodge. And they wanted to take the free tour.

I heard the visitors walking around the kitchen and living room, which is all a big, open space, commenting on this or that. It's funny; I didn't hear them say anything about the complete travesty my house was, with the laundry basket on the living room couch, shoes absolutely everywhere, dirty dishes piled in the sink full of now-cold, barely soapy water, and random papers cluttering the dining table. They must have assumed we'd staged the Lodge to look like a regular family lived there or something—ha ha, what a clever thing to do!

Kitchen drawers were opening and closing—the Lodge tour directions they'd picked up at the Merc said that was permissible, after all—and my heart was beating a mile a minute. My body was starting to feel waterlogged, and the bathwater was getting cold. When I'd first heard the pounding at the door about ten minutes earlier, I was sure whoever it was would eventually give up and leave. I sure didn't think they'd keep knocking, and I most definitely didn't think they'd wind up in my house. And in my wildest dreams, I couldn't have envisioned what happened next.

I heard footsteps getting closer, and one of the voices tried one more "Hello?!?"

Then one of her friends said, "Oh, there's one of the bedrooms!" The instructions also said bedrooms were on the tour.

I could hear them approaching the threshold between the hallway and my room, and I knew I had to do something drastic. There was no way I could leap up and grab a towel in time to cover myself up and graciously tell them they were in the wrong house—oh, and introduce myself. *Hi, ladies! Nice to meet you. So glad you enjoy my cooking show on Food Network! I'm sorry, but the Lodge is up . . . that way.*

So I panicked, pulled my chin to my chest, and belted, "*You've got the wrong house!!!*" in the deepest, most frightening man voice my body has ever produced.

All three ladies shrieked and exclaimed, "Oh my God!!! We're so sorry, sir!!!" Their shoes clomped quickly on the floor as they exited the front door and ran out the way they came. I was still lying motionless in the bathtub when they ran past the window behind me to return to their car. I felt terrible that I hadn't been more hospitable. I'd panicked! And again . . . I was naked.

Once I heard their vehicle peel out of our driveway, I finally felt it was safe to get out and dry off. My heart was calming down a little bit over the whole scenario—not that I was scared of the kind visitors, just that it was a very strange, awkward situation. I hope they're reading this today, and I hope they will accept my apology for not just coming out and facing them (in my robe, don't worry!).

On a side note, I'm kind of impressed that my male voice was so darn convincing. They called me "sir," after all! I'm waiting for just the right moment to use it on Ladd and the boys. Maybe the next time we say grace at dinner . . .

Dogs, Dogs, Dogs

The ranch where we live actually belongs to the dogs. We humans are just guests here.

The very first dog Ladd and I ever had was a Basset hound named Rufus. I'd innocently stopped by Bad Brad's Barbecue to pick up some brisket for dinner one evening, and there was someone sitting in the parking lot, giving away Basset hound puppies. It was all over for me, of course. Rufus was very lazy and grumpy, and my brother-in-law Tim took him for rides on his light turquoise Harley. I'd had a Basset hound when I was a little girl, and Rufus awakened all the low-energy, stinky love that I remembered from the old days—and set the stage for Charlie, the most beloved dog of my entire life, who would come many years later.

Suzie was a Jack Russell terrier—the other end of

the motivation spectrum—and we got her when my girls were babies. She was the sweetest, most intuitive dog I'd ever seen, and she hated all men. She'd go from cuddling under my neck to snarling her teeth if my boys (or, again, Tim) walked into the room. She was hopelessly devoted to me and my girls . . . until my father-in-law, Chuck, convinced her to go for a ride with him on his horse one day at our farm. After that she was his dog for the rest of her life, hardly able to leave his side. Suzie was the only dog Chuck had ever felt a connection with, and he was the only man she ever loved—a beautiful thing to behold.

We had a chocolate Lab on the ranch named Bob. He was not right in the head and always needed to be carrying in his mouth either (a) an empty Dr Pepper can or (b) a large log. Strangely, he would never touch a Sprite can or Coke can—it always had to be Dr Pepper. And he was always dragging off our firewood; one time Ladd found one of our logs three miles down the road. Bob thought horses were dogs, and he thought cats were rabbits. He snorted but never barked. Maybe he thought he was a pig. Species confusion was an issue with Bob. He was the least intelligent dog I've ever known, but it was part of his charm.

Nell, our Border collie, was obsessed with soccer balls to the extent that she destroyed them. She didn't mean to destroy them—again, she loved them. But she would lie on them and chase them and hug them and kiss them and call them George, to paraphrase the abominable snow bunny—and she'd carry them in her mouth, which almost always resulted in a puncture. Have you ever loved something so much that you hurt it? That was Nell and soccer balls. I'm kind of glad they were in Nell's life, to be honest. No telling what kind of chaos would have gone on if they hadn't been.

I want to talk for a minute about stray dogs, which were plentiful given that we lived in the country. There was Buster, a beagle mix who beat up two of my dogs the day he showed up at the ranch, but then decided to stay for a year after that. He was a sweet dog at heart and made amends with the dogs he'd wronged on our homestead, but then one day he was just gone—he'd clearly decided to move along to his next stop. And that's something I've learned about many stray dogs! They're either so grateful they finally found a home and they stay forever, or they really just think of you as an extended-stay hotel and eventually check out. Buster checked out, but that's the life he chose. Everyone has their own journey.

Birdie, a heavily pregnant stray bird dog, showed up at our little house the year after we were married. I was heavily pregnant, too, so we nested together, Birdie and I. I turned our yellow brick garage into a birth-ing center, complete with hay bales, blankets, and all the food and water she'd need to have a comfortable multiple-puppy birth. I even planned to be her mid-wife and birthing partner . . . but right before she had the puppies, she left, and I never saw her again. An-other vagabond dog for my memory book. I hope she told her children about me.

Then there was the Great Dane that showed up at my back door one day when it was storming and Ladd and the kids were all gone for the day. He was so tall, I thought he was a Peeping Tom for a minute, and then I thought he was a horse. Once I determined he was nei-ther, I let him into our mudroom and wrapped him in a very large blanket. We fell in love and spent the whole afternoon getting to know each other, but when Ladd got home that evening, he said we couldn't keep him.

"Why not??" I cried. "Look at him—he's so happy here, and he can keep me company on long, lonely days."

"But you have five other dogs," he quite correctly pointed out. "And I didn't know you were lonely."

"I'm keeping him," I said defiantly.

"You can't," he replied.

"I'm older than you," I reminded him.

"You can't keep him, because . . . ," he began.

"Yes, I can," I interrupted. "You're not the boss of me."

Ladd took a deep breath and exhaled slowly. "You can't keep him because he belongs to my cousin Joe," he explained. I guess Ladd recognized the Great Dane, who'd wandered a little over two miles from his cousin's ranch until he finally happened upon our back porch.

"We could just not tell your cousin Joe?" I suggested. Ladd laughed, then loaded the big guy onto the back of his feed truck and returned him to his rightful home. I wasn't actually kidding; I didn't understand why he had to go back to Joe's. I thought it was very rude of Ladd not to allow me to keep him illegally.

Walter's still with us, and he's a big lug of a Basset hound—perhaps the biggest big lug of a Basset hound that ever lived. When Walter was very young, I let him outside to go to the bathroom and five minutes later, a torrential storm hit—including golf-ball-size hail. Poor Walter started running away from whatever was hitting him over the head, and kept running until it stopped hitting him. We didn't find him until the middle of the next day—three pastures over (about a mile from the house), lying down and taking a nap. Poor Walter had to be wrapped in swaddling cloths and comforted for two weeks, and to this day destroys the house if it even sprinkles outside. That's what I get for putting him outside right before a hailstorm in 2011!

It's probably obvious that dogs have factored prominently in our lives—but no dog in my past (or, I'm certain, future) has ever made a dent in my heart like Charlie, my late Basset. I got Charlie "for my family" one Christmas, but he and I linked souls on day one. He was my constant companion and my friend, and became a cult figure on my blog because of the sheer volume of content I devoted to him. I took pictures of him sleeping. I took pictures of him eating. I wrote stories about his inflated sense of self-worth and his paws, which smelled exactly like Fritos. He was incredibly lazy and emotionally manipulative. I would sometimes lay individual Li'l Smokies breakfast sausages right in front of his nose when he was napping and count the seconds until he woke up. (My dad is so proud of the college education he provided me.) Charlie was a complete nutjob and I was an even bigger nutjob, so we were the perfect pair.

Charlie wouldn't get up from a nap unless he heard Ladd's spurs jangling through the house; then he'd snap to attention and follow him out the door. He loved me for the dysfunctional interpersonal connection we shared, but he loved Ladd for the constant activity.

He'd ride in Ladd's feed truck, help him gather cattle, and keep the horses in line (at least that's what he told himself). He thought he was a cattle dog, and to be honest . . . he was close. Then he'd come home and cuddle with me.

When Charlie was almost nine, he was diagnosed with lymphoma. I wasn't the least bit prepared for this and prayed for him to have more time to be a ranch dog. And because of the great care he received right after his diagnosis, that's exactly what he got to do. He got well enough to chase rabbits, herd cattle, and get showered with love and Li'l Smokies for almost another year before he started going downhill again.

As he got sicker, I prayed for the discernment to know when the right time would be to end his suffering. After all, how do you know when a Basset hound isn't feeling well? How do you know when a Basset hound is lethargic? Their middle name is lethargic. But one Sunday in late January, it became crystal clear that the time had come, and our local vet came out to the house so Charlie Boy wouldn't have to leave the ranch. The girls and I were there, but Ladd and the boys couldn't stay; it was too sad for them. His death was peaceful and quiet, except for my sobs . . . and I cried for a month over all the memories of the best dog a family could ever, ever have. He was the dog of a lifetime for me, and I'm so grateful he was a part of our lives.

Yeah, he was a nutjob. But he was my nutjob.

Dogs are a gift from Heaven, and we don't deserve them.

Dogs and Cats
on Drummond Ranch

Dogs
(in no particular order)

* Charlie
* Duke
* Lucy
* Walter
* Lady
* Nell
* Annie
* Rufus
* Gus
* Henry
* Hamilton
* McCormick
* Buster
* Sam
* George
* Hooker
* Bob
* Birdie
* Susie
* Jett
* Scout
* Nandy
* Rusty
* Fred
* Presley
* Cocoa
* Maggie
* Professor
* Charlie (he's worth a second mention)

Cats

* Kitty Kitty
* Kitten Kitten

Maybe I'll switch to cats for the rest of of my life . . .

Cowboys Are Real

~

A cowboy, by definition, is a person who works on a ranch and takes care of land and cattle. Cowboys often live on the ranch they help care for, and as such, they can become a significant part of the family. This is certainly the case on Drummond Ranch, and after many years of living among them, I can tell you that the cowboys you see in movies and TV miniseries are absolutely real.

Cowboys look the part. They wear sturdy jeans, which many of them starch, and from the cowboy hat on down to the spurs on their boots, their outfits display durability, flexibility, and undeniable style. People often ask why cowboys don't just wear gross old T-shirts to work when they know they're going to get covered by mud and manure, and there are two very good answers for this. First, T-shirts are hot, sweaty, and uncomfortable, as the knit fabric sticks to the skin. Woven shirts, on the other hand, breathe and wick away sweat much better. But aside from that, a T-shirt is entirely too casual and not at all appropriate for most cowboys to wear to the office—and the ranch absolutely is their office. They want to give their work the respect they feel it deserves, so they dress the part. Our cowboy Josh (we call him, appropriately, Cowboy Josh) wears a wild rag, which is basically a patterned silk kerchief, tied around his neck. Wild rags are for warmth and protection from the elements, and they look mighty spiffy. His little boy, Taos, wears one, too.

Cowboys love animals—not just the livestock they take care of but also the scruffy, mixed-breed doggies on their porch. Cowboy Josh had a pit bull–boxer mix named Hooker; he found her hungry and pregnant, wandering in a pasture one day. He took her home and she became his most loyal dog—and is one of my top five favorite dogs that's ever existed on Drummond Ranch. Cowboy Josh also loves *my* dogs, and we have a shared custody arrangement with our canines— sometimes they like to toggle between our two houses, depending on where the leftovers are better. (The dogs are mostly at my house.)

Cowboys cuss like truck drivers, and because of this,

a mother on a ranch has to understand that from a very young age, her kids will occasionally shout out expletives they've heard in the cattle pens. Some of these expletives are quite advanced, and curbing this habit in her children may take a little more time and patience than normal. Don't worry—the kids will be just fine. Cowboy cussing isn't usually pointed at anyone or used out of anger; it's just woven through their speech like a fine twine.

Cowboys are big brothers. The summer after Alex's freshman year of college, she brought a group of friends home to the ranch for a weekend, and all ten of them (a mix of boys and girls from various urban areas) piled into one of the ranch pickups so Alex could take them on a driving tour. As they headed down the road, Alex noticed Cowboy Josh's vehicle heading toward them and she was immediately excited, as she'd hardly seen him at all in the year since she'd left home.

"Oh, that's Cowboy Josh!" Alex told her wide-eyed friends. "He was like a big brother to me growing up." She couldn't wait to introduce them to this special person in her life. The two vehicles stopped, and both Alex and Josh rolled down their windows.

Josh looked at Alex with a huge smile and hollered, "You're an asshole!!!"

Turns out Josh had sent her text messages to check

on her a few times while she was at college that first year, and she'd neglected to respond. He wasn't about to let that go unchecked. No self-respecting big brother would. Her friends died from laughter, of course, but it hardly fazed Alex. It was nothing new to her.

Yes, cowboys are big brothers, uncles, and god-fathers to the kids on the ranch, and they're fiercely protective, sizing up potential love interests with more scrutiny than even the parents. My girls have always said they were never concerned about Ladd approving of someone they were going to date—it was Cowboy Josh they were worried about. Alex never wanted to bring her now fiancé, Mauricio, to work cattle with the crew, because she knew Cowboy Josh would put him through the wringer as he tried to evaluate whether or not he was worthy of her. Also, cowboys are huge tattletales: If they see one of the ranch kids getting stopped on the highway for speeding, or if they hear of one of the ranch kids drinking beer at the lake Friday night, or if they hear a rumor involving one of the ranch kids—which is bound to happen, considering cowboys also happen to be enormous gossips—they will snitch to the parents immediately. They're watchdogs, and they aren't going to keep any secrets if they think the kid needs to get knocked back on course.

Cowboys are gentlemen. For all the cussing and tattling and ribbing and hollering, you'll be hard-pressed to find a more chivalrous lot. They call a lady "ma'am," whether she requests it or not, because it's simply ingrained in them from birth. They say thank you when home-cooked meals are set before them—a home-cooked meal, by the way, is the avenue to a cowboy's soul. Cowboys open doors for females, which some consider an antiquated practice, but which feels like a privilege if you're the lucky recipient. And somehow, even though they let the colorful language rip when they're working with their bosses and the kids, they're able to flip the switch and turn it off when ladies are present. Which makes you wonder why they couldn't just turn it off in the cattle pen, too—but I think cowboys should be allowed to be themselves while they work.

The cowboys I've known through the years, from Big John to Cowboy Josh, have been cowboys their whole lives and do not desire another path for themselves. They get up before daylight, they live in their feed truck and on their horse, and they take good care of animals. It isn't a glamorous life they've chosen. Or . . . maybe it is. Maybe watching the sun rise on horseback is the greatest kind of glamorous life. You get the sense that if they were ever plucked out of their cowboy careers, they'd be in unfamiliar territory. I haven't seen a lot of cowboys who've changed directions and gone to an office job. It would be like putting a stallion in a shoebox.

That's something no one wants to see!

Cowboy Colloquialisms

Here are some gems from the cattle pens.
(These are some of the tamer ones.)

"It's rainin' like a cow peein' on a flat rock."
Translation: It's raining hard.

"All hat, no cattle."
Translation: All talk, no action.

"You're windy."
Translation: You're exaggerating.

"Go piss up a rope."
*Translation: I'm not interested in discussing it
    any further.*

"He's tighter than Dick's hatband."
Translation: He's cheap.

"He's luckier than a three-peckered billy goat."
Translation: He's very fortunate.

"He's worthless as tits on a boar hog."
Translation: He's quite unproductive.

"It's darker than the inside of a cow."
Translation: It sure is dark outside.

"It's colder than a witch's tit."
Translation: It's freezing.

"He's not smart enough to pour piss out of a boot."
Translation: He's not smart.

New Territory

Pawhuska vs.
the Hamptons

*I*t was the most incomprehensible turn of events that resulted in me, a regular gal with no official culinary training, winding up with a cooking show on Food Network. But life is a crazy roller coaster, and right or wrong, good or bad, it happened in 2011. And speaking of incomprehensible: It's still happening! I'm inching close to a decade of shooting *The Pioneer Woman,* and between this, writing cookbooks, and cooking for my family, I can't get away from food no matter how hard I try. (Update: I don't really try.)

Here's an interesting piece of TV show trivia: The production company that films my show is mostly British. Five times a year they fly from London, England, to Pawhuska, Oklahoma, and spend three weeks on my turf, filming me cooking in the kitchen and Ladd working on the ranch, where—let's face it—both of us are at our best. By now, many years into our gig together, the TV crew has become part of our family. We love them all. That said, for the first couple of years of filming my show, there was a bit of a learning curve.

This British production crew is the same company that films *Barefoot Contessa,* Ina Garten's well-loved Food Network series—a series, by the way, that's filmed entirely in and around East Hampton, New York. By the time my show began airing, my British crew already had several years of filming with Ina under their belt. So this means that the first two years we worked together were a continual learning experience for them about the many ways in which Pawhuska, Oklahoma, is not the Hamptons.

Rachel, the producer, was enamored with Oklahoma from the moment she arrived to film my pilot episode. She'd had little experience with the United States apart from New York and California, and she found the unbridled beauty of the tallgrass prairie—and the strong western culture—utterly captivating. Her head whipped around at every Ford pickup that drove past. Her eyes widened in childlike excitement when a cow made a noise. And hearing both the cowboy drawls and the spurs jingling and jangling was almost too much for her English soul to take. She fully embraced her new adventure in Middle America, and her smile was a mile wide. Her enthusiasm for the state in which Ladd and I had grown up was both refreshing and infectious.

Then filming began, and I started cooking. And I found that something as simple as chicken-fried steak would sometimes require a thirty-minute explanation.

"So when exactly does the chicken come into play?" Rachel would ask in her refined English accent.

"Oh, it doesn't," I'd explain, laying a piece of cube steak in seasoned flour and pointing to the marbling. "It's steak."

"How fascinating!" Rachel's voice would sing as she'd focus her eyes on the food. "So you call the steak . . . "chicken" . . . in this scenario?"

"No, it's still called steak. *Chicken-fried* steak," I'd explain. "It's just steak that's fried like chicken."

"So it tastes like chicken but it's actually steak," she'd say. "I see!"

"No," I'd begin. "It tastes . . ." And usually I'd just give up.

Similar exchanges would transpire in the coming months over things like cream gravy, boxed cake mix, pancake syrup, and fruit cocktail. And don't get me started on Velveeta. Velveeta almost shut down production for a week, because that's how long it took me to adequately explain it to my new English friends. And don't get me wrong—I love a beautiful gourmet meal! But in Oklahoma, Velveeta is its own food group.

Rachel fell in love with the romance and drama of country life. My sister, Betsy, visited the ranch during one of our early shoots, and when she asked Rachel if she was liking Oklahoma, Rachel's response was almost operatic. "Oh, yes!" she exclaimed. "Isn't *everything* just *beautiful,* and isn't *Ladd* just *dashing* in his *hat* and his *chaps!*" Her gestures were as grand and full of wonder as her voice. Betsy just stood there scratching her head, trying to square the Ladd Rachel was describing with the brother-in-law she'd known for years.

Rachel would pitch show ideas to me. "I was thinking," she'd say, an enchanted look in her eyes, "that we could follow you to the *mah-ket* [market] and film you as you browse the *pro-dyoos* [produce] and the bakery." She was surely picturing Ina, hand-woven wicker basket on her arm, strolling around a local Hamptons grocery shop for bundles of watercress and fresh-baked brioche. I'd tell Rachel that sure, she was welcome to come to the store with me . . . it's called Pawhuska Hometown Foods, and the baskets are made of red plastic and say "Best Val-U" on them in scratched-up white letters. The floors are linoleum and the bakery is brought to you by Sara Lee. There's a whole aisle of

Velveeta. But yes, you're more than welcome to film it! It'll be a hoot.

Another idea Rachel proposed was that during an evening I planned to have my sister, sister-in-law, and mother-in-law over to film a girls' dinner, it might be fun for a second cameraman to film Ladd and his brother Tim taking the kids on a picnic at the creek—a tale-of-two-dinners type of thing. She imagined a vintage quilt upon which Ladd, Tim, and the six children would all sit as they nibbled on tasty treats contained in (here we go again) a hand-woven wicker picnic basket.

There were just a few problems with this dinner-at-the-creek scenario: First, Ladd and Tim have never been on a picnic in their lives and probably never will. If they aren't working on the ranch, they want to be inside in the air-conditioning, out of the elements. Furthermore, the grass is full of chiggers, especially in the evenings, and they would never, ever sit in it, even with a vintage quilt as a barrier. To top things off, Rachel imagined that after the picnic feast, the men and the kids might go for a little swim in the creek. I could just picture Ladd's glistening abs illuminated by the evening sun as he slowly removed his snug white T-shirt (like in my Soloflex poster in high school) . . . and I cracked up at the thought. Not to mention the snakes: "Have you ever heard of water moccasins?" I asked Rachel. I wasn't sure if *Lonesome Dove* had ever aired in the UK.

Eating outside (or "al fresco," as my British friends like to say) was a frequent theme when it came to early episode ideas. Setting a lovely table in the garden was something Rachel thought would be a beautiful thing for viewers—until I showed her that a garden in Osage County is comprised of overgrown tomato plants, scary-gigantic zucchini, and sunflowers missing their blooms because someone didn't shut the gate to the horse pasture. And then there's the matter of the sustained thirty-mile-per-hour winds on an average, pleasant day. *Al fresco? Heck no!*

One thing we *do* have in Pawhuska that they *don't* have in the Hamptons is cattle ranching. Through the years, Rachel and crew have gotten to witness such agricultural excitement as large-animal vets reaching inside cows' rectums, male calves getting castrated, uterine prolapses, and cowboys hollering and cussing to beat the band. And the cameramen have kept rolling the whole time, maintaining the utmost professionalism— although I'm sure there've been times they've wanted to run screaming back to England . . . with maybe a pit stop in the Hamptons on the way home.

Yes, Rachel and crew have slowly assimilated to

ranch life through the years and have truly become part of our family. They love us and would do anything for us. We feel the same about them. Still, tornado warnings sound, the power goes out, the septic tank backs up, the dogs bring dead raccoons to the porch, the crew gets flat tires, and there are all manner of pests—from spiders to rats—that make their time here more than exciting. In fact, when I compare the social media posts of the crew when they're filming with Ina to posts when they're filming with me, it really paints a complete picture. Soft waves hugging the shore of Montauk, New York, a brilliant orange sun rising in the distance . . . versus a close-up of a hairy tarantula consuming a moth on my torn, rusted screen door.

At least their work isn't monotonous!

Behind-the-Scenes Trivia from My Cooking Show

✳ The first season of filming, we used 131 pounds of butter. These days, it's more like 75. (My jeans aren't smaller, though!)

✳ Todd was six when *The Pioneer Woman* began airing. He's sixteen now!

✳ It used to take one and a half days to film one episode. Now it takes a day. (When my kids film the show, it takes half a day!)

✳ There are about twenty-five people on our regular crew. (Just four people on my kid crew!)

✳ British people call the trunk of a car the "boot." One time they asked me to put the casserole in my boot and I was very confused.

✳ British people call digging in "tucking in." One time our director asked one of my dinner guests to go ahead and tuck in . . . and he looked down and tucked in his shirt.

✳ There are enough groceries to make four passes of each recipe I make, in case something burns or doesn't turn out quite right.

✳ We donate leftover groceries to our local soup kitchen.

✳ On a Christmas special in 2013, I accidentally wore two different green earrings, one in each ear. I didn't know it until the special aired.

* My least-favorite recipe I ever filmed for the show was a chicken strip pizza. I used frozen chicken strips and topped the pizza with coleslaw, pickles, and special sauce. It was absolutely awful, but because it was the end of our last shoot day, we had to move forward with it. I figured it would look better on TV when it aired. I was wrong.

* My favorite recipe I ever filmed for the show was lobster mac and cheese with my girls. I demonstrated how to remove raw meat from a lobster tail, and the mac and cheese was so delicious.

* During long shoot days, our sound guy, Martin, calls out crossword clues between takes and we all try to be the first to shout out the answer. The crossword book is from the UK, though, so there's a lot of trivia I don't know. (No fair!)

* Once I made a four-layer chocolate birthday cake for Ladd on the show and stashed it in the fridge to chill. It fell over, and the fridge has never been the same.

* Cowboy Josh dated a member of the production crew several years ago, and he visited her in London. He wore his cowboy hat and was asked for autographs on the street. (It didn't work out between the two of them!)

* When there are shots of my truck driving down the road, sometimes I'm not the one driving it.

* My director, Olivia, is married to my close-up cameraman, Matt. They had their first baby together during the course of the show!

✳ Ladd has scared me with a rubber snake nine times on the show.

✳ I've scared Ladd with a rubber snake nine hundred times on the show.

✳ At a campout show, Todd (age ten at the time) passed gas loudly on camera. The cameramen had to keep their composure and keep rolling, but I saw their bellies shaking from laughter.

✳ In the first season of my show, I accidentally dropped my microphone in the toilet. (I told the sound guy right away.)

Left in a Man Cave

When Alex left for college, I was a mess for months. The meltdown actually began in the spring of her senior year of high school, when I started realizing that everything she was doing was happening for the last time. The last soccer game, the last class, the last dance. I became teary around March of that year and it didn't get any better leading up to August, when we drove Alex to Texas A&M to begin her college experience. Please feel sorry for Ladd for enduring that drive back to Oklahoma, because he had to listen to Paige and me wail and sob the entire seven-and-a-half-hour journey home. And the sobbing didn't stop when we arrived back on the ranch. Our boys, Bryce and Todd, had stayed with Ladd's parents when we took that trip, so the three of us returned to a dead-silent house.

Paige looked at me, eyes still puffy, and said, "I miss Alex." We both started crying again and didn't stop for a month. Again, please feel sorry for Ladd. That poor man has been through a lot.

So acute was my pain over my first child leaving home that I feared things would never be right in the world—or certainly in my heart—again. But slowly, Paige, the rest of the family, and I began to adapt to our new normal, and we slowly got used to being a family of five instead of six, at least on a day-to-day basis. Paige got through her sophomore year, her junior year, and then her senior year of high school, and during that summer before she left for college, rather than feel the abject dread I'd felt with Alex, I just enjoyed every minute with her. To my relief, it seemed that the pain I'd felt when Alex left home had just been a onetime thing, and now that I'd exercised that muscle of mourning, I could handle the emotions this time.

I figured wrong.

Ladd and I drove Paige to college early one Wednesday morning, three years after we'd done the same with her older sister. We moved her into her dorm without a hitch. We walked around campus, bought her some college gear, and had a nice late afternoon lunch at a local café. But when it came time for Ladd and me to leave, it hit me like a freight train—my little Paigie Girl wouldn't be coming home with us. It was as if we'd just been playing around, pretending that we were taking her to college, but it was never actually going to happen. It hadn't felt real until that very moment. "Well, Mom . . . ," she said, flashing a little smile and reaching her arms toward me, "I love you." She grabbed me in a hug.

The whole bottom dropped out. My throat swelled, my nose stung, my chin quivered, and the tears started pouring from my eyes. I grabbed her tight and sobbed uncontrollably. "No," I cried, making absolutely no attempt to calm my daughter's possible fear and trepidation or to put on a brave face. "No, Paigie! I can't go home without you!" I could tell she was crying, too, but it was definitely more out of concern for her blubbering mother's mental well-being than anything else. Ladd put a reassuring hand on each of our shoulders, possibly trying some hybrid of prayer and a Vulcan mind meld—anything to get these two women in his life—especially his wife—to stop crying, which always completely unnerves him. Ladd can make a fifteen-hundred-pound bull go in the exact direction he wants, but he's powerless to stop a female's tears.

Ladd almost had to physically help me into the

pickup, and I gave Paige a final wave as Ladd slowly pulled away. And oh, the floodgates . . . they opened again. I'm trying to make it sound funny, but it really wasn't. I was devastated, empty, completely destroyed at the idea of my beautiful Paige being gone from our house and apart from my world. She was such a flurry of daily activity and energy, a type A personality that kept our house alive. I loved Ladd and the boys and all, but I just couldn't imagine how daily life was going to continue without Paige there running the show. I terrorized Ladd the entire three-hour drive home with cries of "I regret every moment I didn't spend with her!!" and "Do you think she's going to forget about me?" and other wails that were impossible for him to respond to in any logical way. This was different, way worse, than I felt when we dropped Alex off at school. At least when we drove home after taking Alex, I still had Paige in my life. On this trip home, I knew I'd have only Ladd, Bryce, and Todd at home to fill the void.

After a couple of days of intermittent crying and feeling sorry for myself for being the only woman in history ever to send two of her daughters away to college, I decided to buck up. I owed it to the men in my life to at least *appear* to be engaged. I started high-fiving them more, talking to them about their upcoming football season, and involving them in dinner requests for the upcoming week. *I can do this,* I thought to myself. *I'll just call Paige several times a day to get me through it, then the rest of the time I'll totally be present for the boys and all their endeavors.* I suddenly had a new attitude. And new hope.

Then school started, and here's a glimpse into what the average day looked like: Got the boys up at 6:00 a.m. so they could get to the weight room. After that, they'd go to school all day, then football practice immediately after. They'd trickle home about 8:30 to 9:00 p.m. every single night. Meantime, Ladd was running the ranch, and I was rotting at home with nothing but two Labs and two Basset hounds (and two thousand mama cows) to keep me company. Oh, I had things to do, sure—cooking show, product line, cookbooks, career, yada yada yada—but it didn't matter. That first week, the silence in the house was strange and deafening.

Monday night on the second week of school, I decided that if I couldn't beat them, I'd join them. I was determined to mold my routine to theirs, getting the bulk of my work done during the day so I could have dinner and charming conversation ready for them when they got home at night. *These boys still need a mom,*

I reminded myself. I brushed my hair, splashed water on my face, and started dinner. I couldn't wait for them to walk in and smell the chicken Parmesan simmering on the stove. I looked forward to telling them about my day, to asking them about theirs. The Bassets and I were fresh out of things to talk about.

Bryce, Todd, and Ladd piled in after nine, washed their hands, and sat down for their late dinner, grunting here and there over how delicious it was. They launched into a lively discussion about who the backup quarterback was going to be that season, and I waited for an opening. Ten minutes later, the chicken Parm was obliterated, they'd finished the quarterback convo, and I saw my chance. "Oh, by the way," I announced, "I'm going to Tulsa to get my hair done tomorrow."

Crickets.

More crickets.

And then the darnedest thing happened. The guys nodded, then turned to one another and continued talking about football. I felt slighted for a second . . . then chuckled to myself, reflecting on how different things would have been if Paige had been at the dinner table that night—Paige, who was always eagle-eyed and tuned in about my and everyone else's whereabouts, schedules, plans, motivations, and intentions. Had she been at that dinner table, my hair appointment announcement would have been met with the following inquiries:

What time are you going?
What time is your appointment?
What are you doing to your hair?
How long will it take?
What time will you be back?
What else are you doing in Tulsa?
And then what?
Can I come with you?
Why not?
Can you reschedule to a day I can go?
Why not?
What is your political affiliation?
What is your mother's maiden name?
I need you to edit this English paper.
You should cut your hair shorter.
But exactly what time will you be back?

There was none of that now. Paige was now fully (and understandably) concerned with her life at college, and the dearth of follow-up questions from the guys in my house made one thing crystal clear to me that night: I now resided in a man cave, one defined by football and ranching, one where deodorant and socks were going to be the main emphases. But rather than fight it, I decided to embrace it and use the previously unheard-of quiet time at home to feed my creativity and work on projects.

Nearly two years later, deodorant and socks are still the focus, and I'm loving being the mom of football players. They still don't ask me anything about my hair appointments, and never notice a single change in my cuts or colors, but that's just fine by me. At least I can come and go without having to answer twenty questions! (I don't even have to answer one question.)

Stayin' Humble

O ver time, I've slowly learned to accept the fact
that I am *technically* considered a celebrity, simply by virtue of the fact that I've had a TV show for
several years and am somewhat of a recognizable person (mostly, I suspect, because of my orange-red hair,
which mostly comes from a bottle these days). Coming
to terms with this has basically caused me to rethink the
entire concept of celebrity, because if I am one, I don't
have a single clue what one is. I'm not being falsely
modest here. It's just that when I hear the word "celebrity," I think of one person: Demi Moore. For some
reason, I have always pictured Demi Moore living in a
ninety-room mansion. I can't explain why this is—it
just became implanted in my mind somewhere along

the way that that's the way she—and all celebrities—live. And since I don't live in a ninety-room mansion (I live on a ranch, which I love, in the house my husband grew up in, which I love . . . and I have manure in my yard, which I don't love), there's no way I can be a celebrity, too. Obviously, my point is that "celebrity" is really just a word, and doesn't speak to any reality about the person or the person's lifestyle, so these days especially, I take it with a grain of salt.

All of this said, I do also recognize that *if* I am a celebrity at all, I'm very low on the celebrity scale. This is not a Justin Bieber situation, in other words. Still, because I have a TV show and cookbooks, there are a few (maybe eleven?) people who know who I am and enjoy what I do, and for that I am nothing but grateful every single day of my life. If I ever have the chance to sign a book or chat with someone who has followed my website, read my cookbooks, used my products, or watched my show, I consider it a tremendous privilege. To be recognized in public or asked to sign an autograph is something that I will never, ever complain about.

One weekend a few summers ago, I had my annual gathering of fifteen high school friends at the Lodge on the ranch. We started having these summer get-togethers in 2008, after our twenty-year high school reunion the year before, because a lot of us hadn't seen one another for many years and we had so much fun reminiscing that night that we didn't want it to end. So we vowed to meet every summer at the Lodge, and by and large, we've stuck to that promise. Since these weekends began, we've seen one another through burying spouses and parents, and one of us (not me!) even had a post-forty baby . . . so the connection we've renewed has been truly special.

During these weekends, we cook, drink wine, and laugh for forty-eight hours straight, and we always go away from the weekend renewed and refreshed. To help this along, I usually arrange for a massage therapist and manicurist to come for the whole day on Saturday so the girls can enjoy some much-needed pampering. This one summer, I decided to up the ante and forgo the tradition of all of us cooking the Saturday night dinner together and instead hired two sushi chefs to come from a restaurant in Tulsa. I thought it would be fun to watch the chefs in action, and besides that, it would allow the girls to really dig in and relax rather than pull together a big meal. The girls were all finishing up their various massages and manis late that Saturday afternoon when the two young sushi chefs showed up. We all enjoyed watching them set up their equipment and get started.

We were a couple of sushi courses in when Tracey, the manicurist, invited me to come sit at her portable table so she could do my nails. I didn't always partake in these spa services during our girls' weekends, as I always wanted my guests to enjoy them first, but Tracey and the massage therapist had ridden from Tulsa together and she had some time to kill. And truth be told, I was game to sit, relax, and have my nails done. My cuticles were tragic, and it was nice to unwind, shoot the breeze with Tracey, and enjoy occasional bites of sushi, which both my friends and the chefs occasionally delivered to me on little plates.

Before Tracey started applying the orange-red polish I'd picked out, she paused and looked at me with a shy grin.

"Can I ask you a big favor, Ree?" she said.

"Sure," I replied. "What's up?"

"Well," she began. "My mom, Brenda, is really a big fan of yours—she watches your show all the time. Do you think I could have you sign a cookbook so I could give it to her for her birthday next week?"

"Oh, my gosh, of course!" I answered, thankful that she'd asked me and taking the book and pen she'd dug out of her tote bag. "I'm happy to!" I opened the book and drew a heart on the title page. *Love to Brenda from the ranch,* I wrote in flowery cursive. *Ree Drummond, The Pioneer Woman.*

Tracey thanked me over and over, then asked me a second small favor: Could I please autograph a separate piece of paper for her niece, who was also a fan? I was happy to oblige again, and wrote a fun message to the little girl. At this moment, one of the sushi chefs brought me a special sushi roll he'd made just for me, and I thought I'd died and gone to heaven. By the time Tracey finished up the second coat of red, the chefs started packing up their gear. The sushi meal had come to an end.

My nails had been drying for about five minutes when the same sushi chef came back to the table where Tracey and I were sitting. He was in his early twenties, and he approached me with the same shy grin Tracey had worn earlier. In one of his hands was a piece of paper; in the other, a pen. "Excuse me, ma'am?" he began.

What a sweet fella. I wanted to make things more comfortable for him, as I could tell he was too embarrassed to ask. I reached out and gently took his paper and pen so I could write my autograph. "So who would you like me to sign this to?" I asked, as I set the paper on the table and prepared to write. I assumed it was an aunt or a sister or his mom, as I was sure the autograph wasn't for him. He wasn't exactly in my demographic.

"Oh, ma'am . . . ," he said with a puzzled expression. "That's the credit card receipt for the dinner," he explained. "I just need your signature."

Yep, just stayin' humble around here!

Say Hi to Garth!

As long as we're stayin' humble . . .

Paige played competitive volleyball her junior and senior years of high school, which meant weekend tournaments were a standard thing. One fall weekend took us to a huge tournament in Dallas, where some fifty teams from the region were competing for the top prize. I watched every game, moving myself from court to court, and the enormous gym facility was filled to the brim with parents just like me.

Out of the corner of my eye, I saw a man—clearly the dad of a competitor from another nearby game—looking in my direction and smiling. I smiled back and continued cheering for Paige and our team, who were well on their way to winning another game of the day. When it was over, as the players and parents gathered their gear and headed to the next court on their roster, the same man approached me with his two preteen daughters.

"Hi," he said. He had very friendly eyes and his arms were around his girls. "I tell you what—my wife would just kill me if we didn't get a picture together." Seems the man's wife had to work out of town that weekend and hadn't been able to go to the volleyball tournament. Also, she was apparently a fan of mine, and he thought a picture of us together would cheer her up.

"Oh, gosh—you bet!" I said, walking over and inserting myself into their little cluster. Paige offered to snap the photo for us, and she took the man's phone and coached us into position. This entire time, the man was beside himself with excitement, saying things like, "She is just going to freak out!" and "This is going to make her day." I was so glad I could be of service to them!

He made sure to have Paige snap plenty of verticals and horizontals so all his bases would be covered, then thanked me for taking the time to take photos with him and his daughters. "You're amazing," he beamed. "And so talented!" I took exception to this description, as I'd never really thought of myself as necessarily talented. A good cook—okay, I could see that. But talented—what a nice thing for him to say!

We chatted for a few minutes about our respective teams and how they were doing in the tournament, then started to part ways. "Thanks again!" the dad said, turning to walk away. "I really appreciate your time!! Wow, this is awesome!" His excitement was so sweet.

"My pleasure," I said, heading out with Paige. "Say hello to your wife for me."

"Oh, I will definitely do that!" he said. "She loves country music—especially yours!"

I put my head down and started walking faster. Paige looked over at me and cracked up.

Just then the man, a good fifty feet away from us, turned back and hollered, "Oh, and say hi to Garth!"

I did my best to avoid him the rest of the tournament. I didn't want him to be embarrassed once he realized his error—or worse, I was afraid he'd ask me to sing a few bars. But I have since wished more than anything that I'd been able to read the text exchange between him and his wife when he sent her the photos of him and (ahem) "Trisha Yearwood."

Just picturing it in my head kept me entertained for weeks.

Bonus Kid

～

We have a foster son now. His name is Jamar. I haven't written or spoken publicly about him much, because for one thing, the state agency that handles fostering has strict rules against posting about foster children on social media, which I get. But mostly, and this is slightly related, I feel protective of Jamar and have always wanted his story to be his own and not fodder for my social media, which is often riddled with silly videos of my Basset hounds running toward the camera in slow motion. Also, I've never wanted to subject Jamar to more attention than he wanted or needed before he had a chance to settle in and get his bearings in our home. We needed to let things breathe!

I'm now writing about Jamar because after more than a year of living in our house, he is an inextricable part of our wacky family, and it's become increasingly strange for me *not* to talk about him. He's eighteen now, which means the state agency restrictions no longer apply—and most notably, he told me he's tired of feeling like we're trying to hide him from the world. He's ready to sing, to dance, to make his debut! Jazz hands, Jamar!

Okay, so that's an exaggeration. What I'm trying to say is, he's cool with my talking about him now, and he thinks it's about time, considering he's been in the family for over a year. So let me take this opportunity to tell you all about my bodacious, bright, brilliant bonus kid named Jamar.

That he came to be our foster son was entirely situational. Fostering a kid was never something Ladd and I pursued or felt called to do, but Jamar's circumstances presented themselves to us in a way we couldn't ignore—so, long story short, all six foot five inches of him showed up at our house one July afternoon, bag in hand, ready to move in. Ladd, who had the initial idea to have Jamar live with us, had met him a couple of times during high school football practice that summer. My boys knew him, too. I, on the other hand, had never officially met Jamar before that day, and our first interaction went something like this.

"Hey!" I said, looking up. (Way up!)

"Hello," he said, looking way down. (I'm five foot nine.)

"So . . . what's up?" I asked.

"Not much," he replied.

"Glad you're here," I said.

"Thanks," he said.

"Cookie?" I asked.

"Oh, yeah!" he exclaimed, staring at the platter I was offering. He took one off the top of the pile. Cookies are always a nice starting point.

Ladd and I showed him to Alex and Paige's room, which I hadn't had a chance to convert from their crystal chandelier wonderland into something a little more in line with an average teenage boy's tastes, but Jamar didn't seem to care. That first night, he went to a rodeo with Bryce and Todd like it was just an everyday thing. We figured we might as well give him a crash course in Drummond recreational activities, and a rodeo was as good a place as any! My boys had recently become friends with Jamar through football—he'd transferred from Tulsa a few months before—and they had a great time together at the rodeo. Jamar even wore a cowboy hat. Things were off to a winning start!

Speaking of a crash course in Drummond recreational activities . . . two days later, Jamar hopped on one of our ATVs and took off down our road. He'd never driven before, so when he saw the vehicle in the garage he thought it seemed like a fun activity. About fifty yards down the road, he made too sharp a turn and wound up tipping over the ATV and badly injuring his foot. A skin graft (yikes) and a tendon repair surgery (double yikes) later, he had to stay in bed for more than six weeks to give his foot time to heal. For a kid with aspirations to a football career, it was a dicey, scary time. I tried to help him see that his accident could have been much, much worse—but this was little comfort to him, considering football was the future he saw for himself, and for the time being that appeared to be in question.

I felt bad for Jamar, being new in our house and suddenly laid up with a foot injury, so I overcompensated by serving him "generous" (oversize) portions of home-cooked food every morning, noon, and night, delivering it to him on a tray with all the condiments and beverages he could possibly need, forgetting to factor in that the dude was lying flat in bed, unable to move much, and expending very few calories in a day. This unfortunate nurturing side of me combined with his robust athlete's appetite to help him quickly pack on thirty pounds (update: which he has since lost!) . . . and let's just say I have officially learned my lesson about portion control for a bedridden patient. Turns out you can't apply the same formula you use with a busy cattle rancher. Sorry, Jamar—my heart was in the right place! (Ladd has given both of us a hard time about this for months and says he can't leave us unattended. I respond that we don't want to hear it, considering he wears the same jean size he wore when I married him.)

Jamar's accident, while terrible, did wind up having an unexpected benefit for our newly modified family: It forced all of us to get pretty darn close, and fast. I changed Jamar's dressing on his foot every day, gave him his medicine on schedule, and checked on him in the middle of the night, sometimes only managing to wake him up, since he's a light sleeper . . . but again, I meant well! Ladd drove him to his doctor appointments and physical therapy sessions in Tulsa, and there were a lot of them. Bryce and Todd helped him in and out of bed, wrapped his foot in plastic before he took a shower, and hung out with him when he got bored. We were all up in Jamar's business, and if there'd been any hesitation on any of our parts to interact and get comfortable with one another, his injury quickly knocked down those walls and gave us all a reason to come together. Jamar had to learn to trust us, which wasn't easy. But again: crash course.

Over the year following his accident, Jamar defied the original (somewhat dire) orthopedic prognosis and, while he has a wicked scar and a heckuva story to tell his kids someday, is back to full functionality. He was able to start playing football midseason and has settled in as a full-fledged member of our family. We've had a few bumps in the road here and there that we've had to address—but the same thing is true with Bryce and Todd, or any teenager, for that matter. In fact, having two teenage boys of our own has turned out to be both a challenge and an advantage during this whole process. A challenge, because Jamar and Bryce are just a month apart in age, and there've been some natural turf wars and personality clashes that Ladd and I have had to referee. It can be tricky, because we're mindful not to make Bryce feel like his whole life at home has changed, but we're also mindful not to default to taking Bryce's side over Jamar's. Bottom line, we make them shake hands a lot.

It's also an *advantage* to have two other teenage boys, because the Drummond house is just one big soup of testosterone and disgusting gym bags, and sometimes Ladd and I just have to throw up our hands and surrender to the chaos and disruption—and I'm not talking about the disruption of adding a new kid to the mix. I'm talking about the disruption of having adolescent males in the house, period, with their arguing and fighting and wrestling and banging around and eating and dirty socks and just the general footprint three humans of their size make. We might as well get all of this over with at once. It's much more efficient that way.

Speaking of eating, here's another unexpected development: For years, I have enjoyed the luxury of being able to stock specialty grocery items in my kitchen, like stevia-sweetened root beer and grain-free crackers, knowing none of the Drummond kids (or, especially, my husband) would ever touch them. But Jamar eats and drinks all my specialty foods! He loves my weird, off-the-beaten-path supermarket items, and I have found myself having to lay down some serious boundaries for the long-term health of our relationship. I explained how very far we live from a store that carries, for example, stevia root beer (Tulsa, the nearest location, is an hour and twenty minutes away), and that during the course of my busy day at home, I might work up an appetite for one and make myself wait an hour or two before I partake. And if I finally decide to go for it and find the last stevia root beer is gone when I open the fridge, I just might burst into tears and have a meltdown—surely he didn't want to have to witness that?!? So we have an understanding: He should feel free to help himself to all the stevia root beer he wants—*except for the last one, because if he takes that one, it will not be pretty!!*

(He laughed as I laid all this out for him. He'd never met anyone so protective of root beer before, and I think he thought I was joking.)

(Nobody better come between me and my beloved carbonated beverages.)

This summer, Bryce and Jamar started fishing together, which always helps bring young men together. Fishing was all Jamar's idea—it's not a common activity in the Drummond family, since Ladd's usually occupied with ranching whenever he's outside, but it reminds Jamar of a lot of good times in his childhood. It turned out that fishing completely transformed Bryce's free time over the summer, and I was so appreciative that I decided I wanted to get Jamar some new fishing gear to thank him for helping Bryce—and all their friends, who slowly started joining the fishing gang—navigate the new world of fishing lures and lines. So very late one night, I went on an online shopping spree, finally deciding on the perfect mega (mega doesn't quite do it justice) fishing essentials set, complete with two poles, a tackle box, and all the lures and rigamarole a serious man of the sea (pond) would need. There were specialty cutters, gadgets, and tools, and I couldn't wait to give it to Jamar.

When the box finally arrived, I laid it all out on the kitchen counter so he'd see it as soon as he walked into the house. As he took in the sight, his eyes got wide . . . then he burst into laughter.

"What's so funny?" I asked.

He picked up one of the poles. "Oh, nothing . . . ," he said. "This was nice—thank you, Mama Ree." He still had a smirk on his face, though; he couldn't really conceal it.

"Wait," I said. "What's so funny . . . tell me!"

"Well . . ." He hesitated. "This is all fly-fishin' stuff."

Turns out, I'd bought him a mega set of the very best *fly-fishing* essentials money could buy! For ranch ponds in Oklahoma. Always read the fine print when you go on late-night online shopping sprees! This is something Jamar and I still laugh about, though . . . which might have made the ill-fated purchase worth it.

I could go on and on about Jamar, my bonus son. He's larger than life, has a hilarious laugh, and is extremely smart—both book and street. He's a great kid who's overcome some difficulties in his life, not to mention a tough accident (and a foster mom who overfed him and unintentionally tried to turn him into a fly fisherman).

Through a ton of determination, Jamar has excelled in football, and he's already received a couple of college offers, with more sure to come in! I'm proud of the kid, and I can't wait to see where life takes him.

I'll be in the stands cheering him on!

Herman

Official training is required in order to be a foster parent in Oklahoma, and because Jamar came to live with us pretty suddenly, Ladd and I were allowed to complete the training after he was all moved in. Ladd the overachiever opted for the online training option and began his coursework immediately after Jamar's arrival. It took him nineteen hours of pretty intensive computer work, including phone interviews with the state coordinator, whose job it was to make sure Ladd was retaining all the important information and perspective. I, on the other hand, opted for the procrastination option, because if I'm going to be sitting in front of a computer, I usually have some kind of work deadline I'm trying to finish, and it's very hard to justify doing anything else. Plus, I quite naïvely (and arrogantly) kept dismissing the relevance of the training because after all, I told myself, I'm already a parent, I've had four kids of my own, and what would I possibly learn in foster parent training that I haven't already encountered in my twenty-plus years of raising children? I mean . . . I got this.

Logically, I knew I was going to have to complete the training requirement, but for the life of me, I couldn't seem to move it off the back burner. I was busy taking care of Jamar in the wake of his foot injury, not to mention being a mom to Bryce and Todd. The boys were deep in football practice by then, so there was a ton of coordination, cooking, and laundry going on. I also had a cookbook coming out, which is always uniquely challenging from a schedule perspective. My excuse game was strong, very strong. But unfortunately, as is the case with most deadlines, they don't just disappear if you ignore them . . . and after I missed the first, second, and third extensions, the state agency called and very politely (and clearly) told me that I needed to get off my bottom and complete the training immediately or they'd have to place Jamar somewhere else.

That got my attention. I did not relish the idea of telling Jamar he had to pack his bag and move because I wasn't able to fit foster training in my schedule. (Egads.) Still, I kvetched and complained to Ladd about the fact that not only did I have to complete the training in thirty days, I now had no choice but to take the training *in person,* which is always my very last choice for anything since I don't like to leave the house. My supportive husband had absolutely zero sympathy for me, considering he'd managed to knock out his training so dutifully three months earlier. He rejected my suggestion that I could just skirt the training requirement altogether by going to live somewhere else, leaving him to finish raising our boys and Jamar by himself. (I was 99.8 percent kidding.)

Because Pawhuska is a smaller community, there wasn't a local foster parent training course I could take in that time frame, so that left my driving to Tulsa for five all-day sessions—again, not ideal from a time and schedule standpoint. But then, a lifeline: the state agency coordinator informed me that if I wanted, I could take the training offered by the Osage Nation, the Native American tribe that's headquartered in Pawhuska, and it would satisfy the requirement since they generally used the same curriculum. Still not relishing what lay ahead, I thanked her and told her I was very appreciative not to have to make the drive.

When I called the Osage Nation to enroll, I was told there'd be other people in the class with me—a little bit of a tough pill for my introverted self to swallow. I'd expected this to be more of a one-on-one instruction, but now it appeared that I was going to have to share a class with other foster parents, take part in group activities, and share my thoughts, feelings, and experiences. Ladd chuckled when I told him this, knowing the private homebody he's married to, and he promised to root for me from the ranch.

On the first day of class, I met my fellow classmates: Herman, a Native American gentleman around my age, along with his mother and eighteen-year-old son. They had just begun fostering a family member's child and were fulfilling their training requirement just as I was. Following introductions and administrative details, we sat down and started our coursework together.

After the first day of class, I told Ladd about Herman, the man I'd just met. There was something about him that had made quite a first impression: He had such a strong but gentle presence, and he very openly shared his fears and vulnerabilities when it came to the fostering responsibility he'd taken on. Even though Herman lives a couple of towns over, Ladd was familiar with his name since Herman and many members of his family had been football players when Ladd played for the Pawhuska Huskies. During our class breaks, Herman and I would shoot the breeze about high school football, his favorite kind of pizza, the fact that we both needed to give up pop, and how both of our experiences were going with our respective foster kids.

As it unfolded, the foster training material really started to open my eyes. It taught me the effects that childhood trauma can have on the heart and soul of a human being, and it gave me helpful tools with which to approach my and my family's relationship with Jamar. But something else happened during training, and it was something I never could have predicted: I became fast friends with my classmate Herman. Along with learning the ins and outs of being a foster parent, I also started learning about Herman's Osage culture, which is absolutely central to his life, and which drove his decision to step in and foster a child. In class he recited Osage prayers, explained the structure of an Osage family, taught us how to play Osage games, and shared his traditions and beliefs, always relating them to the lessons we were covering in our coursework.

Without meaning to, I'd catch myself staring, positively transfixed by Herman, the person, the soul. Sometimes when he shared his stories and experiences, tears would well up in his eyes, which in turn made them well up in mine. Even though I was only there because I'd been a procrastinator, here I was, receiving a firsthand account of what it truly means to be Osage. I felt like the luckiest person alive, and to top it off, I'd made a new friend.

The last day of class was bittersweet. Herman and I shared a hug and exchanged phone numbers. He told me I was family, and I could feel the tears starting to form. He invited me to sit on his family's bench at the Osage dances—an incredible honor that I don't take lightly. We've kept in touch ever since, and my heart lights up anytime a text appears on my phone with the name "Herman" at the top. He tells me that my family and I are in his daily prayers. I tell him that he and his family are in mine. I don't remember a time (with the exception of ballet camp as a girl) when I developed such a deep friendship so quickly. It feels beautifully preordained!

Yes, life is wild. A year and a half ago, I never could have predicted that there would soon be a fifth kid in our family . . . and I certainly didn't think I needed another friend, let alone a kind, sweet man named Herman. But despite my tendency toward putting things off and my desire for things to stay the same, I learned a powerful lesson: Sometimes you only have to open the window a tiny bit to let the breeze blow through. Between Jamar and Herman, the events of the past year have been a crazy, holy wind!

A Funny Thing Happened
at My Cookbook Signing

I've released six cookbooks (as well as children's books and a love story!), and have had more than two hundred book signings. It's a wonderful way to meet amazing people, and I've never had a bad experience . . . though there've been a small handful of interesting moments.

For my most recent cookbook, I'd had three back-to-back signings over three nights. Typically during my signings, I stand at a high table as each person in line files through. We take a photo together first, then I sign their book and chat with them for a minute while the next person in line gets ready to come up. A great rhythm usually kicks in and takes over, and I often prompt each person in line with phrases like "Come on up!" and

"Let's take a picture together" as I welcome them forward and put my arm around them for the photo.

After a while, this can start to seem a little repetitive:

"Come on up, let's take a picture together!"
"Come on up, let's take a picture together!"
"Come on up, let's take a picture together!"

But for each person it's their first experience in line, so it never bothers me, and it helps to make people more comfortable about walking up to my table.

On this third night, a lone fella was next in line—his number was probably 225—and when it was his turn to come up I smiled and said my usual "Come on up!" He did exactly that, then, as I reached out my arm to welcome him, I said, unintentionally, "Let's take a shower together!"

He paused and stopped walking, clearly trying to process my suggestion.

And because brain synapses are a living, breathing thing, this has happened to me more times than you'd think. One time I said, "Come on up, let's say a prayer together!" The person actually said, "Okay . . . ," and bowed her head.

To a grandma and granddaughter, I said, "Come on up, let's take a bath together!"

Sometimes I get very tired.

An unrequited high school crush of mine came to one of my book signings with his wife. I hadn't seen him since high school, and he looked exactly the same. I was surprised to see him, and his wife was gorgeous. As we spoke and caught up on life since high school, I started sweating. Then I tried to mentally talk myself out of sweating, which made me sweat more. By the time my old crush and his wife said goodbye, I had sweat dripping down my forehead and sweat beads on my upper lip, and the back of my neck was drenched. As I watched the couple walk away, the next person in line asked me if I was okay and handed me a Kleenex out of her purse.

I can't imagine why he never dated me.

At my various book signings over the years, I have signed:

* Books

* Dinner plates

* Pie pans

* Arm casts

* Cowboy/cowgirl boots

* A wheelchair

* A purse

* Autograph books

* Cell phone cases

* Wooden spoons

* Caps

* Palms of hands

* A forehead

* A forearm

I was once asked to sign a woman's décolletage, but I politely declined. I told her I had way too much respect for Billy Idol to tread into his territory.

(I was very honored to be asked, though!)

At one of my very first book signings, I was sitting at a standard-height table and speaking to people as I signed their books. A young couple approached the table and stood on either side of me.

"We're newlyweds," the guy said, looking at his beautiful wife.

"Oh, how sweet!" I smiled, opening the book and beginning to sign my name.

"We absolutely love your recipes," the young lady said. "We cook them together all the time."

I loved hearing this. "Thank you so much for telling me that," I replied. "I'm so glad you're enjoying them!"

Just then, the young groom leaned in and lowered his head closer to my ear.

"We like to cook them naked," he said, without laughing or cracking a smile.

He stood up and I realized that because I was sitting, I was about eye level with both of their nether regions. I had nowhere to run to and my cheeks felt flushed.

"Oh . . . I'm so glad!" I replied, which was a really awkward thing to say. I handed them their signed book and they said goodbye, strolling away arm in arm.

I'll bet they made one of my recipes naked together that night. I've always wondered which one. (Probably something involving buns.)

A Drummond Family Quiz

(See page 335 for answers.)

1. What wildlife is *not* found on Drummond Ranch?
   a. Badger
   b. Bald eagle
   c. Wolf
   d. Mountain lion

2. True or False: Bryce has been offered a football scholarship.

3. How long is the gravel road between the main highway and the Drummond house?
   a. ½ mile
   b. 1 mile
   c. 5 miles
   d. 50 miles

4. Who is Alex engaged to?
   a. Mauricio
   b. Miguel
   c. Matteo
   d. Manuel

5. What do the kids call Chuck?
   a. Gramps
   b. Pa-Pa
   c. Poppie
   d. Grumps

6 . Which of the following is *not* a Drummond dog?
   a. Walter
   b. Duke
   c. Lucy
   d. Ted

7 . What did Ree do with the (frozen) top layer of her wedding cake?
   a. Celebrated and ate it with Ladd on their one-year anniversary
   b. Gave it to the friend who caught her bridal bouquet
   c. Dropped it when she was leaving the wedding reception
   d. Ate it at home alone one day when she had morning sickness and couldn't think of anything else to eat.

8 . Who is six foot one?
   a. Alex
   b. Paige
   c. Bryce
   d. Ladd

9 . If Ree and Ladd had had a fifth child and it was a boy, what name was at the top of Ladd's list?
   a. Valentino
   b. Ashley
   c. Bull
   d. McKenna

10. True or false: Ladd and his brother Tim call each other "Slim."

11. How many calves are born on Drummond Ranch every year?
    a. 500
    b. 1,000
    c. 5,000
    d. 25,000

12. True or False: Ree's vehicle is a pickup.

13. True or False: Ladd competes in rodeos.

14. Approximately how many Food Network shows has Ree filmed to date?
    a. 50
    b. 150
    c. 300
    d. 1,000

15. True or False: Ree doesn't know how to saddle a horse.

My Idea of a Good Time

I t's nice to be the age I am, because even though I don't necessarily have the same skin elasticity, waist size, or energy I had when I was younger, I'm more sure than ever of what I want, don't want, like, dislike, long for, avoid, crave, can do without, and need. I wouldn't trade the mind and perspective I have now for the teeny jeans I wore years ago—actually, I would if that were possible, but it isn't, so I'm glad to have the mind as a consolation prize! Most valuably, I've found that when the choices I make for work or even recreation cause me to veer too far away from the things that satisfy my soul, I start to unravel, get knocked off balance, run out of steam, and hit a wall. When I think about things that feed me, it's usually not a trip to a dream destination or some spiritually monumental experience that I seek. It's often a food or a person or a feeling that makes me know I'm headed in the right direction. So on any given day, here are the things that make me tick.

Wake up early. While 3:45 a.m. is a little too close to nighttime for me, I'm happiest when I get up between five and five-thirty in the morning, as long as I remember not to look in the mirror while I'm brushing my teeth, because it can be quite jarring. Not that I necessarily need to look glamorous for myself when I get up in the morning, but sometimes the deep crevices and matted nature of my hair make me seriously wonder what I dreamed about—not that I can remember my dreams since I sleep so deeply these days. And by the way, I snore now, which Ladd likes to tell me a couple of times a month. I deny it, of course, and he responds by telling me, "It's cute," which we all know is a lie.

But morning! It's my favorite. The promise of my super-tall, sweetened, creamy iced coffee . . . the knowledge that I'll be there to watch the sun rise . . . the excitement of the dogs when I go out on the porch to greet them . . . time on the couch with my coffee and Psalms and a little quiet prayer time . . . and just knowing, even for the first hour or so, that I have a jump on the day and might have a fighting chance to get through my entire to-do list before nightfall (which I definitely won't, by the way, but I don't know this yet). It's a uniquely delicious feeling. I like sleeping until seven every once in a while, like the third Sunday of the month or something. But any more often than that throws me off.

Stay home all day. The idea of not having to get into my vehicle and leave our homestead during the course of a day is something that causes my insides to do cartwheels and jump for joy. That feeling is actually a kind of fuel for me, as it causes a giddiness that isn't there on days when I have something I have to go do—whether it's filming or getting a haircut or going to a meeting in town (or going out of town). I've figured out that I am very susceptible to interruptions in momentum, and when my momentum is disrupted, it requires a certain kind of energy to get it back. Imagine that my momentum is a pile of leaves, all raked together and tidy. A sudden breeze comes and blows the leaves all over the yard. Raking them back together is exhausting, and that's how I feel when I have to head out among the English, to quote the movie *Witness*. I tell Ladd that if it weren't for church and the occasional work obligation, it's actually disturbing how many months on end I could stay home without batting an eye. (Who knew this gloat would actually be tested this year? Even though I hated the reasons, I felt fortunate that my inherent hermit tendencies helped me during quarantine.)

Dogs everywhere. I simply must have dogs, on my porch and in my life. Right now I have six; I'd be happy with fifteen. They're dopey and goofy and loving and affirming; they have the complete run of the ranch twenty-four hours a day . . . but somehow they're never more excited than when I go outside and tell them it's time to go for a walk. They act like they've been caged their whole life and their savior has just shown up— and I'm always like, "Dudes. You can go for a walk any ol' time you want!" Then they look at me and do a massive head tilt, and I just crack up and feel whole again. Yes, I have to have dogs in my life. (Not in my bed, since Ladd isn't that kind of guy. But it's probably just as well.)

Lots of solitude. I grew up believing I was an extrovert. I believed this because people always told me I was. They said I was the life of the party and made people feel at ease, which I guess was true. But I'm so grateful I finally came to understand that what I actually am is an extroverted *introvert*, and the only reason I've ever been able to be the life of the party and make people feel at ease is that I've spent weeks beforehand *not* doing that. And when I look back at my younger years, though I remember plenty of fun times and parties with other humans, I also remember the times I reveled in sometimes staying home when my friends went out, and how much I loved holing up and watching *Gilligan's Island* all by myself. I have a distinct memory of a group of my brother's high school friends coming to the house one day when I was fourteen and asking me if I ever left the house, because they only ever saw me watching *Gilligan's Island*. Even back then, I knew I needed to preserve my internal resources in order to thrive in social settings. I am absolutely that same person today.

Sushi. I hardly ever have it. I pretty much always want it. About two or three times a year, I get sushi from a restaurant in Tulsa and take it home so I can chuckle at the irony of eating sushi on a cattle ranch. It is absolutely my idea of a good time, and here's part of the reason why: I go bonkers with wasabi now, smearing it on each and every piece before dunking it in soy sauce, because redheads can handle spicy food more than the average person (see page 88). The heat from the wasabi clears my sinuses and triggers endorphins, which makes me feel happy from head to toe. Ergo, sushi makes me feel happy from head to toe. If I were putting together my perfect day, sushi would be a part of it.

Uninterrupted work time. This is first cousin to staying home all day and sibling to solitude, but to me, the promise of being able to work, think, and create for days on end is something I always crave. It could be posting a detailed cooking video on social media, brainstorming ideas for my next cookbook, developing products, or any number of other projects that allow me to keep my creative side alive. Sometimes I like just being able to sit, write a blog post, and crack myself up. When I'm at home alone, I even laugh out loud at myself. (Well, and even when I'm not home alone.)

Go to Colorado. Okay, I realize I don't like to leave the house. But Colorado is an exception. It feels safe to me, the air is medicinal, and I associate it with family memories and a feeling of getting away from the hustle-bustle . . . even though the hustle-bustle is our isolated cattle ranch. I walk around town and look at fancy European ski jackets that I'll never buy, and I love the fact that I pant walking across the room for the first couple of days I'm in the mountains. Makes me feel alive! Also, I go to a church there that makes me cry happy mountain tears, which are the very best tears. The mountains themselves are actually my church.

Get a massage. I don't get them often, because I'd have to drive an hour and a half to Tulsa to get one, and then I'd have the hour-and-a-half drive back to the ranch, and then what would be the point of getting a massage if you have to spend three hours in the car? But in my head, my heart, and my dreams, I wake up, have my iced coffee, say hi to the dogs, then go get a massage. That's what Demi Moore did in that ninety-room mansion I always imagined she lived in (since she's a celebrity, after all—see page 303), and it always seemed like the one thing I'd have if I could have anything in the world. Given the choice between a personal chef, a chauffeur, a house cleaner, a glam squad, and a massage therapist, I'd absolutely, 100 percent choose the massage therapist.

In the absence of an actual massage therapist, last year I bought "my family" (air quotes) one of those big kahuna automated massage chairs for Christmas. I didn't get out of it for the entire month following Christmas. Ladd would come home midmorning and I'd be in the massage chair. Ladd would come home midafternoon and I'd be in the massage chair. Ladd would ask me if I was ready to turn in at night and I'd say, "In a little bit. I have to get in the massage chair." I started to actually monitor our family tracking app so I would know when Ladd was about to be home, so I could get out of the massage chair and act busy. I felt like he was catching me cheating. (It's an ongoing affair, by the way.)

Limit travel. Someday I will see the world. I'll travel to the faraway places I've never been and tour, explore, and eat my way across the continents. When the kids are grown and living their lives, I'll be eager for more global experiences. But for now, today, my heart wants to stay close to home. I've had enough business travel in recent years to know that the schlep and the time away from my recharging station takes a weird toll on my equilibrium. Plus, I hate unpacking, and after a few months of travel, this can start to cause problems. So for now, with the exception of blessed (and geographically convenient) Colorado, Imma hang close to the ranch and get my kids raised.

The Real Housewives of anywhere. They are my friends. Not in real life, but in my head. I've watched the Real Housewives for so long, I'm completely invested in our friendship. When the Real Housewives are on TV, my friends are in the room, but I can be an introvert and not have to expend energy socializing with them. I understand that this sounds extremely dysfunctional, but I am being completely honest. I love you, Ramona. Call me, Vicki.

Laugh with old friends. Speaking of friends, I do get together with actual in-the-flesh old friends once a year (see page 304). They've known me since elementary school. We spend two days together reminiscing, catching up, acting decades less mature than we should, cooking, drinking wine, and laughing. The laughter comes from the belly and often progresses to tears, and I don't know the science behind the health benefits of this kind of laughter . . . but I certainly feel them kick in. One weekend a year is all we need. It sustains me and gives me a wicked ab workout.

Hang with my children. Despite my need for alone time, and despite my occasional weariness with frying endless amounts of bacon, I love being able to enjoy my kids in their old age (well, their teenage and young adult years). I still mother them (girls) and boss them around (boys) and probably drive them crazy (girls and boys) from time to time, but I love being able to hang with them and soak up the people they're growing into. I don't have to be around them constantly and am fine with them doing their thing and living their lives, but when we *are* all together, I feel like the lights are a little brighter in our house. And I love the evolution of the sibling relationships—the natural bonds and alliances that form. They're all my favorite dang people.

Help wherever I can. I try to find opportunities to make a difference, whether in Pawhuska or beyond. I have to wrestle with my comfort zone sometimes and resist the tendency to help on my terms (i.e., not in person) or in ways that are only easy or comfortable for me (i.e., not in person) . . . but I'm always reminded that when I push through that, it's when the good stuff really happens. Giving is a muscle, and I try never to let atrophy set in, but it's a daily process. (Such a football mom thing to say!) Ladd is much better at this than I am; when it comes to helping, he's not afraid to dive into uncomfortable places. And that is one reason I love him.

Try to do my best. I check in with myself a lot—about my thoughts, words, and deeds. My faith requires that I approach any thoughts of "me" with humility, and I try to regularly put my own actions under the microscope and make sure I'm doing (or at least trying to do) the decent thing. My biggest lesson in recent years has been to listen—and when we're asserting our position or defending, we can't do that. This has allowed a world of perspective and understanding to flood in and spill over. I'm grateful for the gift of listening. It's a tough one to learn. (I'm also not the best at saying "I'm sorry" . . . it's on my "do better" list.)

Watch the sunset. Sunrises may be my best friend . . . but sunsets are my secret lover. Whether I'm cooking or working or doing laundry or taking a walk, if I see a gorgeous sunset forming, I try to stop and breathe it in.

Breathing in a sunset sets fire to your soul!

Be with Ladd. When I'm with Ladd, things simply feel more right than when I'm not. As my mother-in-law, Nan, demonstrated in her own marriage, I try to be a soft place for Ladd to land, and to dust him off when he comes in tattered and torn from work or just life. The catch here, though, is that he does the very same thing for me, stepping in and lightening the load if there's any burden he can take off my shoulders. He's got my back, and a handy bonus is that he's cute.

Our love language, Ladd's and mine, is quality time, and while both of our work schedules can give us a run for our money, we cling to our evenings and protect them with our lives. We have become Mother and Daddy, settling in our respective chairs in the living room, TV on in the background and feet up on an ottoman. In fact, we've become who Ladd's grandparents, Ruth and Fred, were back around the time he and I got married. I used to see them on their chairs and chuckle that they spent their evenings this way, sipping on soft drinks over ice and commenting to each other about whatever TV show they were watching. *Such old-people business,* I'd think. *What a quiet, boring existence.* But now I see so clearly what's magical about it. It's a sacred time, a precious time, a recharging station for our marriage.

(Even though Ladd totally hogs the remote . . .)

Acknowledgments

To all of you! Thank you for being there for me, whether you've watched my show through the years, read my blog in the old days, or just picked up this book for a fun, light read. We are forever friends now!

To my incredible editor, Cassie Jones Morgan: "Thank you" doesn't begin to express my gratitude! Your patience, wisdom, perspective, and encouragement are second to none, and I can't imagine working on a book with anyone else.

To Susanna Einstein, for believing in me for more than ten years! Thank you for your steady, kind, reassuring support.

To everyone at William Morrow who helped make this book happen: Jill Zimmerman, Liate Stehlik, Ben

Steinberg, Tavia Kowalchuk, Anwesha Basu, Bianca Flores, Rachel Meyers, Lucy Albanese, Pamela Barricklow, Mumtaz Mustafa, Yeon Kim, and Andrew DiCecco, and to illustrator Joel Holland. Thank you for making everything come together! (And for being patient with me.)

To my beautiful friends, who understand me and love me anyway. ☺

To my parents, for always loving me, supporting me, and cheering me on. Love you so much.

To my father-in-law, for treating me like a daughter. Love you, Pa-Pa.

To my whole extended "fam damily"—Tim, Missy, Caleb, Halle, Stuart, Betsy, Elliot, Patsy, Michael, and Doug . . . and the other Doug. Thank you for being a part of my world. I love you all!

To my children, Alex, Paige, Bryce, Todd, and Jamar, for being the greatest kids in the universe. I love you so much.

To Mauricio! Welcome to the family! We love you and we're gonna have fun.

To Ladd, for bringing adventure, excitement, love, and Wranglers into my life for twenty-five years. So glad you're mine.

HARPER
LARGE PRINT

We hope you enjoyed reading
our new, comfortable print size and found it
an experience you would like to repeat.

Well – you're in luck!

Harper Large Print offers the finest in
fiction and nonfiction books in this same larger
print size and paperback format. Light and easy to read,
Harper Large Print paperbacks are for the book lovers
who want to see what they are reading without strain.

For a full listing of titles and
new releases to come, please visit our website:
www.hc.com

HARPER LARGE PRINT